THE ANATOMY
OF CYBER-JIHAD

CYBERSPACE IS THE NEW GREAT EQUALIZER

JAMES SCOTT (SENIOR FELLOW – INSTITUTE FOR CRITICAL INFRASTRUCTURE TECHNOLOGY)

DREW SPANIEL (RESEARCHER – INSTITUTE FOR CRITICAL INFRASTRUCTURE TECHNOLOGY)

EXPERT RESEARCH CONTRIBUTED BY THE FOLLOWING ICIT FELLOWS:
- Malcolm Harkins, ICIT Fellow (Cylance)
- John Miller, ICIT Fellow (Cylance)

ICIT | Institute for Critical
Infrastructure Technology

The Cybersecurity Think Tank

ICIT BRIEFING:
THE ANATOMY OF CYBER-JIHAD

JUNE 29, 2016
WASHINGTON D.C.

Join ICIT experts as we discuss the findings of this publication and identify solutions to protect our critical infrastructures and our way of life.

http://icitech.org/event/the-anatomy-of-cyber-jihad-cyberspace-is-the-new-great-equalizer/

Institute for Critical Infrastructure Technology

The Cybersecurity Think Tank^{TM}

www.icitech.org

ISBN-13: 978-1-535193-36-8

CONTENTS

ABOUT ICIT: THE CYBERSECURITY THINK TANK

The Institute for Critical Infrastructure Technology (ICIT), a nonpartisan cybersecurity think tank, is cultivating a cybersecurity renaissance for our critical infrastructure communities. ICIT bridges the gap between the legislative community, federal agencies and the private sector through a powerful platform of cutting edge research, initiatives and educational programs. Through objective research and advisory, ICIT facilitates the exchange of ideas and provides a forum for its members to engage in the open, non-partisan discourse needed to effectively support and protect our nation against its adversaries.

www.icitech.org

PART 1

ICIT BRIEFING:
THE ANATOMY OF CYBER-JIHAD

CYBERSPACE IS THE NEW
GREAT EQUALIZER

INTRODUCTION

Over the past few years an abundance of rhetorical bravado has been creatively exhausted by the legislative community and law enforcement to expedite legislation that will protect us from a future cyber event so catastrophic, so devastating, that it could only be described as "THE" Cyber Pearl Harbor. The fact is that, the Cyber Pearl Harbor that many seem to be waiting for has already occurred in the embodiment of the Office of Personnel Management breach. The devastation to our counter intelligence, general population and federal landscape as a whole is so profound that the damage of this breach has yet to be fully calculated. Compounded by the Anthem breach, over 100 million Americans have their most intimate personal details in the hands of a foreign APT, most likely controlled by China, for multi-generational exploitation, blackmail and surveillance. Strangely, an incident that should have had Americans protesting in the streets, was quickly swept under the rug and vanished from conversation.

While federal stakeholders have been quietly sweeping America's Cyber Pearl Harbor under the rug and China uses the aforementioned stolen information to construct detailed dossiers on Americans, a new adversary has emerged which defies geographic lines, statehood and political parties. This new malicious actor is consumed with the religious extremism of the crusades and armed with a full arsenal of technological weaponry that can bring an attack directly to the doorstep of every organization, man, woman and child in the United States and Europe. Cyber-Jihad has quickly arrived on the scene and will only continue to grow and hyper-evolve. As a well-funded adversary, Cyber-Jihadists can easily outsource the more sophisticated attacks, purchase potent zero days, infiltrate and map networks and exfiltrate and manipulate data from America's virtually unprotected Internet of Things.

From Al Queda to Al Shabaab, from Boko Haram to ISIS, this Cyber Caliphate flourishes in the techno nutrient rich, binary soil of the Internet and continually reinforced via graphic imagery and unique story telling in publications such as Dabiq and Kybernetiq. The rapid success of the Cyber-Jihad movement has been expedited via magnification of xenophobia, powerful and organized propaganda and the targeting and recruitment of social outcasts from the American Midwest to the Streets of Paris and London, and religious zealots who make easy recruits for carrying out cyber-attacks as part of the collective and lone wolf initiatives.

Vindictive upstarts and script kiddies are able to rapidly hone their skills under the tutelage and assistance of hackers operating ISIS's Cyber Help Desk and big targets become easy prey with step by step, point and click cyber-attacks in this ideologically driven crusade. Making use of readily available content and hashtags, Twitter, Facebook, YouTube and Vimeo become powerful mechanisms of weaponized social media. Even the lower level actors such as Boko Haram are upgrading their exhausted 419 scams with ransomware, RaaS and MaaS, which flourish due to the fertile population of cyber hygienically lackadaisical computer users globally.

Cyberspace is indeed the new great equalizer, the Internet of Things is the new battlefield, anonymizing tools are the new weapons for stealth, malware is the new air strike, vulnerabilities are the new focus of attack, and robust zero day arsenals are the new symbols of supremacy as the old world order is technologically toppled and supplanted by the new.

Until now, it has been fairly easy to categorize malicious cyber-actors as State Sponsored APT, Hacktivist, Mercenary and Script Kiddie. The chaos and religious extremism in the middle east has spun the Cyber-Jihadist into existence. These actors possess select characteristics of each of the above while injected with the religious fervor of the crusades. This new actor uses technological means, to bring terror, chaos, and attack to the door step of every American, European, and global infidel. Cyber-Jihadists are the newest threat facing the U.S. and our Allies.

Cyber-Jihadists, a perseverant variant of cyberterrorist, are especially complex adversaries. They do not solely seek to exfiltrate valuable data or information. Cyber-Jihadists are motivated by complex ideologies that oppose the very existence of Western culture. These groups do not obey the unspoken conventions that restrict the activities of criminal and nation state threat actors. Cyber-Jihadists do not fear reprisal and in many cases, their ideology actually encourages collateral damage. These threat actors seek to cause chaos, disrupt operations, and inflict devastating impacts on organizations in every critical sector. Groups such as ISIS already possess the capacity to acquire the means to conduct crippling cyberattacks. In the Energy sector and Financial sector, attacks have already begun. Unless organizations react to preempt the threat, it is only a matter of time before a cataclysmic breach results in a dire impact on the nation.

1 | POTENTIAL CYBER-JIHADIST ORGANIZATIONS

Terrorists differ from traditional soldiers in that they are not bound by the laws and conventions that society expects a civilized military to follow. Since ideology transcends nationality, members of these militant organizations can hide in the midst of their enemies. Historically, terrorists have been known to exact brutal and ruthless manifestations of their ideology or will on innocent populations and noncombatants. Jihadists are uniquely willing to devoutly adhere to a set of guiding principles while sacrificing as much as necessary to achieve a goal.

Similarly, Cyber-terrorists are not bound by the ambiguous code of ethics and practices followed by other digital presences, ranging from hacktivists to law enforcement.

Information is a profound equalizer. It allows small groups to compete on the same level as criminal syndicates and governments. Because the internet, when used appropriately, facilitates anonymity, cyber terrorists are able to tailor their operations to their desired amount of exposure. Subtle attacks can be used to gain information and resources, while publically claimed attacks can increase notoriety and fear. Cyber-terrorists are willing to attack any target to cause chaos or to realize a gain for their cause. The information and wealth acquired from their attacks may be transformed into weapons in the physical war fought by their organization. ICIT Fellow Todd Helfrich (Anomali) contributes, "Hackers motivated by ideology can be some of the most dangerous since their timeline and persistence to accomplish their objective can be measured in many months or years and they are not motivated by financial gain so they may take risks others won't." In many ways, belief is more powerful than demonstrations of force or strength. After all, that is the reason that nation states imbue a sense of patriotism in their citizens. Cyber-Jihadists are willing to go to extreme lengths to serve their beliefs. They do not fear public exposure, unless it compromises an operation, because their real-world activities are already illegal enough to place them in the sights of many militaries and law enforcement entities.

Since the advent of the internet, terrorist groups have been transitioning to cyber or cyber- physical organizations because the world wide web expands their web of influence wide across the world. The rate at which a group adopts new technology is based on their resources and their membership. Groups with greater access to technology and funds and with younger members develop faster than other groups. Even though the jihadist groups may share some specific goals, such as religious beliefs, the formation of a global caliphate, and opposition to their enemies, each major jihadist group differs in its ideology, structure, and capabilities.

AL QUEDA

Al Qaeda founder Osama bin Laden relied on charisma, fatwas, and rhetoric to rally militants to his cause. After bin Laden's death in 2011, Ayman al Zawahiri assumed control of the organization. Al Qaeda does not directly manage the daily operations of its factions. Zawahiri does not claim to have direct hierarchical control over Al Qaeda's vast network. Instead, he works with the core leadership to centralize the organization's messaging and strategy. The core leadership includes a Shura Council, and committees for military operations, finance, and information sharing. Leaders communicate through the respective committees. Members are required to consult with the core leadership before conducting large-scale attacks.

Al Qaeda supports a caliphate, in principle, but it views the global caliphate as a long-term objective. In the early 2000s, affiliates proposed establishing caliphates in Yemen and Iraq, but bin Laden believed that the attempts would ultimately fail. The leadership believes that foreign powers, such as Americans, must be expelled from the region in order for a caliphate to succeed.

According to cloud security firm, BatBlue, Al Qaeda has used technology and the internet to distribute officially sanctioned propaganda since the 1980's. In the 1990's, the group began to use the internet for secure communications between members. Most Al Qaeda communications are encrypted or obfuscated in some way. When emails or messages cannot be encrypted, operatives attempt complex codes or operational strategies to obfuscate the message. Security firms have observed Al Qaeda communications using steganography or using hidden links in apparent spam emails between members. BatBlue asserts that some Al Qaeda operatives worked for big software firms, the military, and the banking industry until around the year 2000. These operatives may possess some knowledge of coding or hacking; however, in recent years, the group has relied on younger, more innovative partner terrorist organizations, such as the Tunisian Cyber Army, whenever it launched cyber-attacks. In February 2015, Al Qaeda announced that it had developed a cyber arm, Qaedet al-Jihad al-Electroniyya, to perform electronic jihad operations under the command of "Yahya al-Nemr" and "Mahmuda al-Adnani".

Al Qaeda remains active on Twitter and video distribution sites; nevertheless, Al Qaeda still does not have the social media presence, recruiting capabilities, or technical sophistication of novel groups, such as ISIS. Al Qaeda maintains its digital following in the region that it controls through online publications and through online communications.

AL SHABAAB

Al Shabaab is a Somalia based militant organization with strong ties to Al Qaeda. Al Shabaab was the militant wing of the Somali Council of Islamic Courts that seized southern Somalia in late 2006 until 2007. Since then, it has continued to fight in southern and central Somalia, relying on guerilla warfare and terrorist tactics. Al Shabaab is not centralized or monolithic in its agenda or goals. It consists of disparate clans; consequently, it is susceptible to internal strife, clan politics, and brittle alliances. It does not appear interested in a global jihad.

The group conducted attacks on Uganda's capital in 2010, a raid on a Nairobi mall in 2013, and an attack on a Kenyan University in 2015. The group was an early adopter of the internet and shares many of the strategies as Al Qaeda; although, it is definitively less sophisticated. The group predominantly uses the internet in a limited capacity to disseminate propaganda, to recruit from external Somalian communities, and to sporadically antagonize its opposition on platforms like Twitter. Occasionally, the group posts online videos and recruitment material in English, Somali, and Arabic. Al Shabaab has also limited its capabilities by restricting use of the internet in the regions that it controls, such as in January 2014, when it banned mobile internet use and fiber optic connections in its operating region. Overall, Al Shabaab's disjointed internet strategy and lack of technical proficiency prevents it from posing a real threat in cyberspace.

BOKO HARAM

Boko Haram is a terrorist organization that strives to establish a militant Islamic state in Nigeria. Founded by Mohammed Yusuf in 2002, the group initially focused on opposing Western education. Initially, it recruited local children through a school that claimed to promote an Islamic education. The children were trained as soldiers and it began launching military operations in 2009 in an attempt to create an Islamic state. Nigeria's security forces responded to the threat and Yusuf and hundreds of his supporters were killed. The group rallied under Abubakar Skekau, who has led since then.

Boko Haram promotes a version of Islam that forbids Muslims to participate in political or social activities associated with Western society. This includes participating in political processes, receiving a secular education, or wearing Westernized clothing (shirts or trousers). It was classified as a terrorist organization in 2013, and it declared a caliphate in the regions it occupies in 2014.

The group was aligned to Al Qaeda until January 2015, when it switched allegiance to ISIS. Afterward, the group's presence on social media and its distributed propaganda materials have become more robust. It is possible that it receives assistance from ISIS in the creation and distribution of its materials. Prior to its association with ISIS, Boko Harem used the internet to distribute propaganda and to conduct unsophisticated online scams to raise funds. The group's social media presence remains inconstant and poorly aligned with its other propaganda. After allying with ISIS, its published videos and photographs began to mirror that of ISIS. Boko Harem has not yet begun to heavily recruit online. Its propaganda is used more to spread fear than to recruit. It is possible that the group raised funds in the past through an advanced fee fraud or 419 scam. Essentially, the scam involves promising a victim a share in greater financial holdings if they provide a forward investment to "free the funds". Security researchers believe that the group still does the 419 scam because it is still profitable for them and because it allows them to target individuals, instead of large organizations or governments. The group has not shown signs of adopting more sophisticated methods of raising funds, such as ransomware. At the time of this writing, Boko Harem does not have a widespread cyber strategy; however, its alliance with ISIS may lead to the rapid development of newfound capabilities.

ISIS

The Islamic State of Iraq and Syria (ISIS), also known as the Islamic State of the Levant (ISIL), the Islamic State (IS) or the Daesh, was originally formed as an Iraqi branch of Al Qaeda in 2004. It has since developed into an independent organization that is more radical in its views and more technologically sophisticated in its use of social media and the internet. In summer 2014, ISIS leader Abu Bakr al-Baghdadi declared a global jihad. He called on all Muslims to join his cause by either travelling to Iraq or Syria or by supporting the jihad locally. The call specifically focused on recruiting technically skilled and sophisticated individuals, such as engineers, hackers, and doctors, to join the cause.

ISIS leader Abu Bakr al Bagdadi avoids public exposure and he relies on ruthless violence to assert his power. Bagdadi is the supreme religious and political leader within ISIS. In 2014, he personally issued the call for all "true Muslims" to join in a global caliphate. The caliph has unchecked authority, but it relies on regional deputies to oversee its regions and manage the imposed administration in each region. The Shura Council can theoretically depose the caliph; however, such an action is unlikely since all members were appointed by al Baghdadi. ISIS also has a Sharia Council and councils who are responsible for security, military affairs, media, and finances. Many of the top administrative positions in the bureaucracy are held by foreign fighters. ISIS keeps detailed records of its operative and it claims to directly control the actions of its fighters and the residents of its territories. Its ability to direct and control its affiliates abroad is unclear. ISIS attempts to govern its territories with an active militia, a court system, school services, and local governments.

Subjects remain loyal out of fear of harsh punishments, such as lashings, stonings, and executions.

When it separated from Al Qaeda in 2014, ISIS seized territories in Iraq and Syria, and declared a global caliphate. It attempted to justify the declaration in the first issue of its propaganda magazine, Dabiq, by outlining steps to ferment local chaos and shaming other jihadist groups that do not attempt to capture and rule territories.

ISIS has a strong online presence that heavily recruits and promotes "lone-wolf" actions through social media. Their radical beliefs are spread by a diverse, unregulated band of digital zealots across conventional social media such as Twitter, Facebook, and Tumblr, and on less conventional channels such as forums and message boards. Members target lonely and misguided individuals, regardless of their initial beliefs, by offering a sense of community and by glamorizing the fight, actions, and lifestyle of the movement. ISIS poses an active cyber threat by working with lone hackers, hacker groups, and by appropriating open source online materials. Some members are technically sophisticated enough to promote the message and culture by defacing websites, social media accounts, and other media channels with text, images, and videos, glorifying the agenda of the group. The technical tools, techniques, and procedures of the group are rapidly escalating as its membership and resources increase. Increases in ISIS online activity tends to coincide with major current events. The group capitalizes off the chaos that it creates, such as launching a major Twitter campaign after the Paris attacks, as well as by turning global events, such as the Syrian refugee crisis, to its advantage.

ISIS encourages young supporters to tweet, blog, and otherwise share their reactions, opinions, and views. The group calls new recruits to conduct domestic lone-wolf attacks using novel mechanisms, such as the hashtag "#FightforHim" following the Paris attacks. The success of the ISIS propaganda campaign is influencing how other groups use the internet. In much the same manner that newspapers' popularity declined in favor of online media, static propaganda publications are declining in favor of robust, dynamic multi- platform campaigns. Their social media campaigns are widespread, resilient, and adaptive. ISIS content is constantly removed from conventional social media; however, they have or had a presence on Facebook, Twitter, Tumblr, Instagram, Friendica, Diaspora, and other outlets. Their videos are edited, clear, and include special effects. Video content has been released on YouTube, IS-tube, Dailymotion, personal blogs, and on other media hosting networks. They have released podcasts and interviews on Ask.FM, Mixir, Paltalk, and other channels. ISIS has also used more conventional media outlets, such as Al-Battar Media, Dawla Media, and Al-Platform Media, to spread its message. Their regular publications, Kybernetiq and Dabiq, feature coherent, well-written content, clear editing skills, and are available in multiple languages. These publications can be found with a Google search, through resilient hosting links on Twitter, on Pastebin, and on JustPaste.it. Much of the content conveyed in these campaigns is defensive encryption techniques and operational security strategies meant to engender a sense of beneficial paranoia in its audience.

Through their social media gauntlet, ISIS has acquired a small, but significant following of technology savvy script kiddies and wannabe hackers. These recruits typically end up as members of the Cyber Caliphate, the dedicated hacker division of the Islamic State. ISIS has also aligned with a few pre-established groups. The Terrorist Team for Electronic Jihad, an anti-Israel and anti-Westerner collective, have pledged support for ISIS. The group mostly attacks websites and operates a few social media pages. The Army of the Electronic Islamic State, with around 150 members, also supports ISIS. The Army has launched cyberattacks against Arab media outlets on behalf of ISIS.

Portions of AnonGhost, a Palestinian hacktivist group, support ISIS. AnonGhost is sophisticated enough to launch DDoS attacks and employ preconfigured tools. In their

#OpIsrael campaign, they flooded Israeli websites with TCP, UDP, and HTTP traffic. The tool was publically released on their Facebook page, featured a YouTube tutorial, and operated through a proxy. Interestingly, in AnonSec's #OpNasa publication, the group, which was founded by former AnonGhost administrator MrLele, mentions AnonSec's opposition to ISIS. AnonSec was revealed to have infiltrated NASA public systems in early 2016 and attempted to seize command of a drone. The insider perspective demonstrates that AnonGhost support for ISIS is not universal within the group. It is likely that some AnonGhost members are native to territories that have been terrorized by ISIS or that they hold ideologies different from the radicals.

Defaced websites are often reconfigured to feature the flag of ISIS and phrases like "Hacked by the Islamic State". The defacements are meant to scare Western businesses and organizations more than recruit new followers. Website defacement often occurs through widely publicized vulnerabilities, such as an outdated WordPress plugin. Those affected range from businesses, to schools, to individual users. By inconveniencing small targets, ISIS creates a sense of fear and xenophobia in the target population that it can leverage to recruit Muslims and social outcasts who are disenfranchised by cultural stigmas.

Screenshots, recordings and lists of defaced and targeted websites have been found on forums, such as Aliyyosh, an Arab hacker forum. Stolen Personal Identifiable information belonging to Israelis and Western and American Jews has also been discovered on the forums. In March 2015, a list of names, units, addresses, and photographs of over one hundred U.S. military personnel, supposedly involved in the bombing of ISIS targets, was posted online. The list did not suggest that ISIS had compromised any secure systems; instead, it is believed that the group created the list from open source information and social media profiles. Since then, ISIS has published similar lists with members of various government agencies, such as a collective 100 employees of the State Department, and of private individuals, such as a list of 3000 New York City residents. The Cyber Caliphate publishes these lists in the hopes that local recruits will conduct lone-wolf attacks on the targets. As with website defacement, their goal is to create widespread fear and xenophobia that will polarize society.

So far, ISIS has dedicated much of its offensive cyber capabilities to compromising and hijacking specific social media accounts belonging to individuals, businesses, and government organizations. Targets have included the Twitter and YouTube accounts of U.S. Military Central Command and Newsweek magazine. In a few instances, ISIS has shown more sophisticated capabilities, such as the use of malware, preconfigured tools, or insider threats. In the former case, ISIS created spear-phishing emails that appeared to oppose ISIS, and sent them to an anti-ISIS group, the Raqqa is being Slaughtered (RSS) opposition group. The emails contained malware that returned the victim's IP address and geolocation information to ISIS.

2 | ANALYSIS OF ISIS AS A CYBER-THREAT

Nephophobia, in psychology, is used to describe a person's fear of clouds (in the sky). Financial institutions have an innate fear of cloud computing, with respect to the sensitive nature of their business transactions.

MOTIVE

Extremist groups such as ISIS aspire to create chaos, inflict harm, and disrupt services in the nations and organizations that they oppose. In many cases, small attacks that incite panic and fear in many members of the population are just as effective as large attacks that embarrass or undermine opposing geopolitical powers. Jihadist groups are increasingly motivated to adopt cyber-defensive capabilities, such as encryption applications and anonymity tools, so that their members can remain undiscovered within the general population and so that their activities remain unknown to opposing intelligence and counterintelligence entities. By developing cyber-offensive capabilities, extremist groups can raise funds, inflict harm from across the globe, gather information about targets, disrupt or dissuade opposition efforts, divert the resources of their enemies, inspire a sense of fear or fame in global populations to establish a brand, and recruit new members through coverage of their activities. Jihadist groups such as ISIS operate in regions where information security may not be built into the culture; as a result, they can use offensive cyber-attacks to identify local dissidents, create economic pressure in target regions, or precede physical incursions.

ISIS and the organizations that support it, have been expressing increasing interest and capacity to conduct cyber-attacks against the Western world. On September 10, 2015, the "Islamic Cyber Army", a predecessor to the United Cyber Caliphate, tweeted, "the hackers Supporters of the Mujahideen configure under the banner of unification in the name of Islamic Cypher [sic] Army to be …[the] working front against the Americans and their followers to support the ISLAMIC STATE Caliphate with all their forces in the field of e- jihad … we also announce for RAID soon targets the Crusader coalition forces electronically, targeting everything…ranging from accounts of recruited, to their banks and their airports. To their nuclear bases." Similarly, on May 11, 2015, Rabitat Al-Ansar, the media department of ISIS, released a video titled, "Message to America: from the Earth to the Digital World," that promised persistent hacking attacks on American and European electronic targets. In the video, the group added that, "…the electronic war has not begun yet. What you have seen before is just a preface for the future. [We] were able until this moment to hack the website of the American leadership and the website of the Australian airport, and many other websites despite paying billions to secure your electronic websites; however, it became easier to hack your websites in a short time. Thus, your security information is in our hands; you do not have the power to fight the Islamic State." The following September, the division tweeted plans to penetrate banks and American government sites on September 11, 2015; though, there it is unclear whether attacks were attempted. Other tweets and qualitative reports of attacks indicate that as of May 2016, the cyber collectives that support ISIS predominantly target websites and systems belonging to government entities, media outlets, financial institutions, and critical infrastructure facilities

MEANS

RESOURCES:

In June 2014, ISIS leadership declared the formation of a caliphate. Since then, the Soufan Group and others estimate that over 27,000 foreign jihadists, from over 86 countries, have travelled to Iraq or Syria to join the extremist group. More than half of the migrant militants originated in the Middle East or North Africa. The recruited extremists were predominately from Tunisia, Saudi Arabia, Russia, Turkey, Jordan, France, Morocco, Lebanon, Germany, and the United Kingdom. In June 2014, ISIS also seized the city of Mosul in northern Iraq and proceeded to push Iraq's army southwest, towards Baghdad, while attacking ethnic and religious minorities in the areas. The United Nations estimates that ISIS killed more than 18,800 civilians in Iraq between January 2014 and October 2015. ISIS is believed responsible for the deaths of at least 4000 Syrians between June 2014 and January 2016. In an attempt to stymie ISIS influence, the United States began launching airstrikes on the Iraqi regions occupied by ISIS in August 2014. So far, over 8277 airstrikes have been launched against ISIS targets in the region. The U.S. led coalition strikes include the efforts of the United Kingdom, Australia, Belgium, Canada, Denmark, France, Jordan, and the Netherlands. In September 2014, a multinational coalition, led by the United States, began airstrikes on the occupied regions of Syria. Approximately 3,791 coalition airstrikes have been conducted against ISIS targets thanks to the efforts of the United States, Australia, Bahrain, Canada, France, Jordan, the Netherlands, Saudi Arabia, Turkey, United Arab Emirates, and the United Kingdom. Russia began conducting separate airstrikes in 2015, targeting terrorist groups such as ISIS, the al-Nusra Front, and other extremist groups; however, some have alleged that Russian strikes have also affected rebel groups who violently oppose ISIS and its allies. The airstrikes have killed at least 25,000 ISIS jihadists in Iraq and approximately 3,914 militants in Syria. As a result of the collaborative multinational efforts, ISIS has lost approximately 40 % of the territory that it held in Iraq and 10-20 % of the occupied territory in Syria. As of April 2016, ISIS controlled territory was approximately the size of Belgium and its leadership is believed to be based in Raqqa, Syria. In January 2016 interview, Colonel Steven Warren remarked "We estimate there's between 20,000 and 30,000 members of [ISIS] operating inside both Iraq and Syria." In 2014 Fuad Hussein, the chief of staff of the Kurdish President Massoud Barzani, gave a more generous approximation of around 200,000 militants. It is likely that including militants in foreign nations across the globe, the number is somewhere between these two predictions, albeit closer to the former estimate. As of May 2016, an estimated 10 -12 million people still live under the control of ISIS forces. An additional 4.8 million Syrians and 3 million Iraqis have fled the region or have been displaced within the countries.

ISIS funds itself with captured Syrian and Iraqi oil infrastructure. Additional funds are drawn from looting, property confiscation, taxes, banks, gains made from grain silos, and the exploitation of other resources of the occupied regions. In October 2015, the U.S.-led coalition conducted airstrikes on vehicles used for pumping and transporting oil at the extraction facilities as part of "Operation Tidal Wave II". Due to the airstrikes and due to ISIS's inability to service aging equipment, it is believed that oil production decreased. On April 7, 2016, the Telegraph estimated that ISIS drew a daily revenue of £1.8 million (~$2.6 million). At an April 26, 2016 press briefing at the Pentagon, Air Force Major General Peter Gersten, revealed that recent airstrikes against ISIS cash sites may have wiped away $300- 800 million of ISIS estimated wealth. An additional $150 million was destroyed a month previous, when an airstrike was conducted against the home of the ISIS finance minister.

Targeting ISIS's resources causes fractures in the leadership of the group and cripples recruitment and expansion efforts. As a result of the growing internal tensions, ISIS may actually be more dangerous because it may innovate under pressure.

ISIS predominately uses social media and the internet to recruit fresh militants for little to no fiscal investment. Its barriers to enter other realms of cyber are low. Given a few laptops, a few thousand dollars, and a few disgruntled technology professionals, ISIS could begin to conduct ransomware or other cyber-attacks to generate additional funds. Software solutions to real world problems are remarkably efficient because software can be infinitely replicated and deployed once purchased. Malware is a software solution that cyber-adversaries employ to raise funds, disrupt services, infiltrate systems, or steal sensitive information. Even if ISIS dedicated some of its resources to recruiting or hiring only a handful of skilled hackers, the damage to critical infrastructure and global financial institutions could be devastating.

Consider the Carbanak group, a small criminal advanced persistent threat group whose attacks against hundreds of global financial institutions between December 2013 and June 2014, resulted in an estimated $1 billion in losses in the first half of 2014. According to Kaspersky Labs, each victim bank lost $2.5 million to $10 million. Overall, Carbanak is believed to have stolen over $1 billion in less than 6 months. Depending on the choice of targets, a localized loss of $10 million to $1 billion to financial institutions in developing countries could result in economic instability and geopolitical unrest favorable to ISIS. The Cyber-Jihadists could destabilize regions prior to invasion or disrupt far-off regions in an attempt to redirect the resources of opposing forces, such as Russia.

Like most APT groups, Carbanak attacks began with a spear phishing campaign. The malicious emails appeared as legitimate banking communique accompanied by attached Microsoft Word (97-2003) documents and Control Panel Applet (.CPL) files. Based on ISIS's multilingual publication, Dabiq, ISIS is already capable of crafting very convincing spear phishing emails. Carbanak's attachments infected victim systems with malware and with a backdoor based on the Carberp malware or contained URLs that redirected the victim to a landing page that delivered the malware in the background before forwarding the user to a familiar financial site. After successful exploitation of an often publically available vulnerability, the shellcode decrypts and a backdoor is installed on the victim host.

The Carbanak backdoor installs and then it re-installs itself into "%system32%\com" as a copy of "svhost.exe" with the system, hidden, and read-only attributes. The initial version (delivered by the exploit) is then deleted. After installation, the backdoor connects to its C2 server through HTTP (with RC2+Base64 encryption) and downloads a file (kldconfig. plug) which details which process to monitor. The kit sets the Termservice service execution mode to auto to enable Remote Desktop Protocol (RDP). The backdoor provides access to the intranet of the victim organization and allows the adversary to probe the intranet for other vulnerable targets and specifically for critical financial systems. Typically, Carbanak infected tens to hundreds of computers before an admin system, with the necessary access, is compromised. If banking applications such as BLIZKO or IFOBS are discovered, then the malware sends a special notification to the C2 server. Attackers then deployed keyloggers, tools to hijack video capture, and screen capture tools to learn as much information as possible about the environment. Often, toolkits log keystrokes and takes screenshots over 20 seconds intervals. Carbanak captures videos at low bandwidth and it uses them to help the attackers develop an operational picture of typical workflow, tool usage, and practices. In addition to training the adversary to transfer money, the monitoring also reduces the likelihood that the adversary will set off behavioral analytic systems. Their remote administration tool, Ammyy Admin, might also be installed on victim systems to ease remote access (the tool is whitelisted by legitimate system administrators in some corporate environments). Carbanak studies the financial tools and applications installed on the victim hosts in order to maximize the potential gain from the compromised system.

Rather than searching for exploits and flaws in the security and financial applications, they monitor the activity of administrators to learn how to transfer money. Currently, ISIS lacks the technical proficiency to conduct an attack of the same sophistication as Carbanak; however, ISIS has some advantages over the small criminal group. Carbanak, as a small APT, must carefully select targets and determine on which systems to spend time. Every wasted hour is a loss to the campaign. The Cyber-Jihadists have more people and more time to spare. ISIS can train dozens or hundreds of members to use malware, infiltrate systems, learn financial tools and procedures, and probe victim networks. Unlike Carbanak, ISIS does not have to worry as much about being caught by authorities. Their members are already wanted by most law enforcement agencies and geolocation attributing cyber- attacks to the occupied region may only promote the fear and paranoia that ISIS publically seeks. In summary, if ISIS acquires a sophisticated enough piece of malware and recruits or hires a small cadre of hackers, it could conduct attacks against critical global institutions with catastrophic cascading impacts.

THE CASCADING IMPACT LEFT BY JUNAID HUSSAIN

The ISIS Cyber Caliphate was formed under a British hacker Junaid Hussain, under the assumed name of Abu Hussain Al Britani. Hussain was known online as "TriCk", the founding member of TeaMpOisoN, a small unsophisticated hacktivist group. TeaMpOisoN was famous for website defacement and denial of service attacks against large corporations and government entities, such as Facebook, NASA, NATO, and the United Nations. Hussain was arrested in 2012 for hijacking accounts belonging to Tony Blair and posting personal information online. In 2013, while on bail, Hussain fled to Syria and joined ISIS.

Hussain was a prominent recruiter within ISIS and it is believed that he is responsible for developing much of their cyber and social media strategies. While "TriCk" possessed adequate technical knowledge, he was unable to launch meaningful cyber-attacks for ISIS, in part because none of the hackers that he knew wanted to work with him after they discovered his affiliation to the jihadist group. Hussain managed to persuade one contact, Ardit Ferizi, also known as "th3Dir3ctor Y," to assist him in obtaining personal information for public release on August 11, 2015. Ferizi, who was believed to be the leader of the Kosova Hacker's Security collective, was arrested and tried for providing the personal information of over 1,500 American government personnel, to Hussain. The information included names, emails, passwords, department or division placement, location data, and phone numbers of 1,500 military and government personnel from within the Air Force, foreign embassies, the Marines, NASA, USAID, and the New York Port Authority. The released information also included the credit card information of several State Department officials and screenshots of private Facebook messages between United States servicemen. A majority of the information disclosed was publically available on the internet and on unclassified systems.

Hussain appears to have failed to recruit any other notable hackers. Instead, he tried to increase recruitment efforts on Twitter and other social media and he began to coordinate the various unsophisticated cyber branches that were sympathetic to ISIS, into the Cyber Caliphate. The series of forums, communication channels, and appropriated cyber- defensive instructional materials, referred to as the "ISIS help desk," was devised under his suggestion. He may have also been involved in the Dabiq and Kybernetiq publications.

Hussain may be responsible for instigating the "lone-wolf" attacks, in which ISIS publishes lists of targets and calls for new recruits in foreign countries to attack them. Lone-wolf attacks are often preceded with a claim that a list of targets was obtained from a hacked database or agency. So far, the lists published suggest that they were compiled using open source information. Even though he was not a key member of the leadership, Hussain's contribution to the cyber capabilities of the terrorist organization made him the third most valuable target in ISIS.

PHISHING WITH EXPLOSIVES?

In August 2015, GCHQ and the US intelligence agencies cracked the encryption on the terrorist communications on the Surespot mobile messaging application. Hussain used Surespot and other encrypted messengers to communicate with contacts and to draw in recruits. An undercover agent sent Hussain whale-phishing email containing a poisoned internet link. When opened, the link delivered him to a landing page with embedded malware. The malware obtained his IP address and used it to geo-locate him before redirecting him to the expected page. The entire process took only a few nanoseconds. After his location was known to allied forces, he was killed in a drone strike on his location.

Junaid Hussain's death was confirmed by his jihadist bride, Sally Jones in the months following the attack. In the wake of his demise, militants hijacked 54,000 Twitter accounts and used the compromised accounts to spread ISIS propaganda. The militants also published a database of the Twitter account owner information as well as mobile phone numbers, names, and other details of individuals located in the United States, the United Kingdom, and Saudi Arabia. Twitter, quickly disabled the infected accounts.

Hussain was replaced by a British-educated Bangladeshi computer expert and businessman named Siful Haque Sujan; however, he too was killed in a drone strike on Raqqa, Syria on December 10, 2015. So far, the United States has limited the expansion of ISIS cyber capabilities by conducting cyber-physical attacks against pivotal members of the organization. ICIT Fellow John Miller (Cylance) agrees, but he warns, "With the rise of ISIS as a cyber power, the concept of nation state proportional response no longer applies. The multiple drone strikes responsible for the deaths of Siful Haque Sujan and Junaid Hussein are proving to be effective in suppressing the immediate rise in cyber capability of this group, however it is not a sustainable long term solution." Since Sujan's demise, it is unclear how well the factions of the Cyber Caliphate are coordinating with one another. The fracture can be seen in the indecision concerning their name. Some factions refer to their collective as the Cyber Caliphate, some use the term Caliphate Cyber Army, and others still refer to it as the Islamic State Hacking Division (ISHD). It may be important to note that while the Cyber Caliphate has vigorously endorsed ISIS, the opposite is not true. ISIS has never claimed ownership of the Cyber Caliphate.

RECRUITMENT

Hussain helped to develop the ISIS recruitment network over a swath of social media outlets and encrypted messaging clients. ISIS is not the first extremist group to rely on social media. Cassettes were passed around in the 1970's. In the 1990's, select Al-Qaeda operations were broadcast on satellite TV. After September 11, 2001, Osama Bin Laden likewise broadcast some speeches via satellite channels. However, modern social media is far more pervasive and ubiquitous than former mediums. Every teenager and most adults have one or more accounts on the various platforms. ISIS and other groups can freely publish videos on YouTube, lectures on Sound-cloud, manifestos on Facebook, and propaganda on Twitter. The defining difference is that ISIS is more effective at social media than other extremist groups. They have developed processes to keep their feeds and links alive when their accounts are taken down and they have even developed Android applications such as "Dawn of Glad Tidings" to distribute their message more effectively.

According to Richard Stengal, the Under Secretary for Public Affairs and Public Diplomacy, by May 2016, Twitter has publically taken down over 200,000 accounts, YouTube has supposedly taken down millions of videos, and Facebook has hundreds of people working to remove ISIS content. Nevertheless, despite the combined opposition of over 60 countries and global organizations, as of 2016, ISIS remains a persistent global threat. ISIS survives by recruiting new fighters into its ranks, from the areas it occupies and from foreign nations. Americans may naively believe recruitment on these platforms to be ineffective or impractical, yet intelligence agencies and the terrorists themselves disagree. In May 2016, the German criminal police and internal intelligence published a study of the more than 800 individuals who have left Germany for Syria or Iraq for ideological motives. In a May 28, 2016 interview with NPR, security analyst Adrian Schtuni estimated that approximately 1000 individuals from the Balkans have recently joined ISIS or Jabhat al-Nusra. He predicts around 5000-6000 individuals have been recruited from Western Europe. Overall, it is believed that ISIS has persuaded 20,000-30,000 recruits to join their caliphate since June 2014. However, some believe that recent airstrikes affecting revenue streams and recent domestic counter-propaganda efforts may have decreased monthly recruiting efforts to around 200 militants per month instead of the 1500-2000 recruits per month estimated last year. ISIS tends to appeal to "poor unfortunate souls" and "troubled youths," with a sense of community and an aggressive ideology. Alarmingly, the stereotypical antisocial, disgruntled youth targeted by ISIS, is also the stereotype for young script kiddies. As it faces increasing opposition in cyberspace and as its seized technology breaks down, technology savvy personnel will increasingly become the most valuable resource to ISIS. It is imperative that opposing forces prevent ISIS from recruiting educated or talented individuals.

Thanks to its publications and strong communication structure, ISIS members exhibit decent operational security and increasingly strong cyber-defensive capabilities. If the group obtains the personnel capable of offensive cyber capabilities, then the threat that it poses to the world will be greatly amplified because it will be able to infiltrate targets' systems, collect information to plan attacks, disrupt operations, and otherwise terrorize its adversaries from anywhere on the globe.

CYBER CALIPHATE

Even though it was not endorsed by ISIS, the Cyber Caliphate is believed to be the coordinated effort of Junaid Hussain. Some contend that the organization is an unaffiliated supporting group, while others believe that the group is a Russian misinformation campaign. The former theory is credible, because Hussain died before the official declaration of unification of the affiliate groups. Hussain was the connection between many of the recruits and teams. It seems likely that some information was lost when he died. The latter theory is based around indicators of compromise discovered in the TV5Monde attacks attributed to ISIS. As discussed later in this publication, it is possible that the Russian APT 28 infected the same system as ISIS and it is possible that APT 28 infected a system and masked their presence by framing the Cyber Caliphate.

In response to his death and in response to increased cyber-attacks from the United States and Anonymous on ISIS, four pro-ISIS groups, the Sons of Caliphate Army, the Caliphate Cyber Army, the Ghost Caliphate Section, and the Kalashnikov E-Security Team, merged into the United Cyber Caliphate (UCC) in April 2016. The UCC is predominately capable of hacking soft targets, such as Twitter accounts, and spreading propaganda or defacing websites. While none of the groups incorporated possessed sophisticated capabilities, their unification has resulted in an increased interest in coordinating and conducting cyber- attacks against govern-ments and organizations. It is possible that the shared coordination will enable the collective to learn more skills and increase their sophistication; however, it is more likely that the Cyber-Jihadists will purchase malware, will rely on malware-as-a- service, or will outsource stages of an attack to mercenary hackers.

PUBLICATIONS

DABIQ:

It is possible that ISIS will draw in new recruits or mercenary hackers through one of its publications. ISIS regularly releases two full colored magazines, complete with feature articles and photo spreads, in a variety of languages. Dabiq is a regular 60 to 80-page publication that promotes the extremist ideology as well as containing editorial pieces about current events. Dead suicide bombers and insurgents are treated like celebrities in a subliminal attempt to glorify their actions for new recruits to emulate. Some articles indicate that the editors pay close attention to American and British politics. Meanwhile, ISIS regularly refer to members as slaves, terrorists, jihadists, and other intuitively derogative terms. ISIS does not fight for freedom or to change the view of the world. To them, they fight in service to vengeful Allah, and they are willing to take any bloody action necessary to fulfill their perversion of Islam. The publication is filled with images of dead bodies and nightmarish brutality intended to shock and awe the reader. The magazine regularly attempts to persuade new read-ers to embark on a "Hijrah," or the trip to join ISIS. Every Western soldier, civilian, or politician, regardless of race, creed, or views, is referred to as a "Crusader." The articles regularly encourage "true" Muslims who can-not physically join the Islamic State to go out and murder the "Crusaders" near them. Most of the hate and vitriol in the articles is directed against Muslims who shy away from or ideologically differ from ISIS. Individuals who conduct lone-wolf attacks against either enemy, such as the two men who attempted to murder people at a Draw Mohammed event, receive full spreads in the magazine. Abdelhamid Abaaoud, a Belgian citizen and one of the planners of the November 13, 2015 Paris attacks, openly provided a detailed account of his travels and intentions in the seventh edition of Dabiq magazine, prior to the attacks. Further, in case the promise of glory fails, violent videos, twitter tags and social media columns aim to entice young readers into the cause through an engendered sense of community.

It is clear throughout the 11 issues of Dabiq, that ISIS believes that a U.S. led invasion is inevitable. In fact, the group desires violent reprisals that hasten such an invasion because they believe that Allah will destroy enemy armies in the Dabiq valley of Syria. Allied airstrikes and United States cyber-attacks harm ISIS in ways that it cannot yet reciprocate. Moreover, the magazine regularly features images and stories praising the allied forces for the influx of weapons, seized through conflicts, into the region.

Dabiq unintentionally reveals that ISIS is financially unstable. A combination of airstrikes on oil production equipment, airstrikes on cash sites, and decreased tax revenue that results from refugees fleeing the areas, has caused ISIS to experience fiscal strain.

Currently, it spends roughly half of its revenue just paying its soldiers. Articles in Dabiq attempt to scare refugees from fleeing the territories by propagating stories of foreign xenophobia or of the deaths of child refugees. Dabiq also features pleading calls for technical and specialized professionals to join the cause. Information Security and Information Technology professionals are included in these aspirational recruits. The more educated professionals ISIS manages to draw into its leadership structure, the more dangerous it will become in its terror campaign against the world.

KYBERNETIQ

Kybernetiq is a December 2015 ISIS publication released in German, which teaches information security and operational security to ISIS militants. The author, "iMujahid" opens the jihadist cyber-war publication saying, "It is very important to us that our brothers and sisters learn the proper handling of software and hardware. Once the West's technological and scientific progress was banished as the devil's work... we tended to demonize the work of the infidels...It is time to learn about its enormous importance of technology and learn how to apply it correctly." The articles contained within include advice on how to remain vigilant when communicating with fellow jihadists, and warnings such as "The enemy is reading with you. Stay vigilant and don't underestimate them." The initial issue explains Open PGP encryption and alternatives to WhatsApp, Gmail, and Hotmail. Readers are instructed to only share information, even with trusted parties, out of necessity. Essentially, the initial issue of Kybernetiq is an introductory course in privacy and information security. The publication is alarming because it poses as a mechanism by which the technical minority of ISIS can train the majority to prevent data loss and potentially to conduct attacks. Imagine the harm that could be wrought if the next issue taught every member of ISIS how to conduct a DDoS or ransomware attack. Even if there are only 20,000 members, the sheer number of attacks could impact an enemy nation state. ISIS militants are, for the most part, devout followers willing to do anything necessary in service to their malformed ideology. Radical zealots are one of the rarest and most terrifying cyber-adversaries. These cyber-martyrs would have no qualms attacking any target in the world, including hospitals, schools, or critical infrastructure facilities, with malware so long as "Crusaders" suffered as a result.

THE ISIS CYBER "HELP DESK"

In November 2015, the media reported that ISIS has spent over a year developing a "24- hour cyber help desk", across a series of forums, applications, and social media platforms, to assist its followers in remaining anonymous and instructing them on basic hacker tools, techniques, and procedures. The campaign is intended to spread the Jihadist message to new recruits, spread greater fear, and increase the number of attacks against foreign nations. The primary function of the help desk was to instruct perspective jihadists in the use of encryption and other secure communication applications to evade law enforcement and intelligence authorities. The group promotes the use of deep web forums and secure platforms to obfuscate their activities so that they can covertly plan recruitment, propaganda, and terror campaigns without worrying that signal intelligence or other indicators will expose their operations.

Supposedly, the help desk is staffed 24-hours a day by at least six senior operatives who possess enough knowledge to answer questions on a variety of technical and non-technical subjects. Observed communications suggest that the core ISIS members behind the help desk possess at least collegiate or masters level training in information technology. Other less technical members, located across the globe, also assist in answering questions in a timely manner. Consequently, a community has formed since last year. The Counter Terrorism Center (CTC), an independent research organization at the U.S. Military Academy at West Point, monitored the communications for over a year and assessed participation based on log-off times and the Muslim hours of prayer. They found that members signed on from across the globe.

The moderators regularly use social media to distribute YouTube videos and tutorials on how to use applications such as Metasploit or Kali Linux to conduct attacks against vulnerable websites and applications. ISIS even communicates instructions, such as "how to not be hacked by Anonymous", across platforms such as Telegram. ISIS relies on these platforms for recruitment and propaganda. Recently, ISIS has favored Twitter and other "more privacy protective" platforms over those owned by Facebook. According to Monika Bickert, who oversees the team that responds to Facebook complaints of nudity, extreme content, or Terrorism, "One thing we've heard time and time again from academics is if you want to find terrorists online or those supporting terrorist ideologies, the best thing is to find their friends. So when we become aware of an account supporting terrorism, we look at associated accounts so we can remove them immediately."

Law enforcement, Twitter, and collectives such as Anonymous, actively attempt to disrupt or take down ISIS accounts in an attempt to erode its influence. Nevertheless, new ISIS accounts continue to appear almost as fast as they are taken down because the help desk now distributes a manual to teach new members how to use login verification options, how to disable GPS tagging on photographs and posts, and how to securely message on the platform.

The CTC obtained more than 300 pages of training documents instructing would-be jihadists in digital operational security. The tutorials and documents are distributed on the forums and through persistent links on social media platforms such as Twitter. One such document was a 34-page operational security manual written by a Kuwaiti cyber-security firm, Cyberkov, for journalists and activists operating in Gaza. The manual details avoidance and secure use of social media platforms, anonymous internet browsing through applications like Tor, and disposable and anonymous email clients. The manual discusses the use of encrypted mobile communication through Blackphone, Cryptophone, or the Silent Circle applications. Further, the guide details how to communicate and send photos within smaller groups (up to 80 people) in a vicinity of 200 meters of less, using the Firechat application, for when an internet connection is not available. The guide covers the use of end-to-end encryption of non-stored instant message applications such as Apples iMessage or Wickr, respectively. ISIS distributed the manual to new recruits in online forums and likely in real world training. The CTC's finding is troubling because it shows that ISIS is now sophisticated enough to recognize its intellectual deficiencies and to locate and appropriate pertinent information to serve its purpose. In this manner, any information security whitepaper, journal, or publication (including this work) may be acquired by the terrorists and perverted to serve their needs.

Over time, the help desk establishes personal connections with perspective recruits through the sense of community and mentorship. ISIS leverages that connection to draw in new recruits and to persuade them to participate in additional recruitment, fundraising, and potentially, even attacks. FBI Director James Comey has repeatedly voiced concerns over ISIS's increasing ability to hide its recruitment and communications in secure or dark areas of the internet. As a result, the FBI and other intelligence agencies must learn and understand how the latest secure communication tools function to understand how ISIS communication is occurring. ICIT Fellow Todd Helfrich (Anomali) confirms, "ISIS and other terrorist organizations have proven their ability to operate in the physical world while coordinating and communicating using new encrypted and pseudo-anonymous channels." The terrorists' ability to migrate to new applications or communication channels faster than law enforcement can understand the applications or can devise a means of data collection, poses a serious problem to national security.

In the age of information, knowledge is power. The advent of the secure and obscure forums that collectively amount to the cyber help desk should worry global intelligence organizations because ISIS now has the capability to educate its zealots in cyber terrorism and espionage. They can now securely coordinate and communicate with one another as fast as information can flow through the wire instead of the previous rate of person-to- person espionage. Their network of voluntary and paid operatives expands across the globe. The leadership of ISIS can gather information, plan attacks, and issue commands without leaving their hiding places. In this manner, an attack conceived in Syria, could be organized, communicated, and implemented in France, the United Kingdom, or the United States, in a matter of hours or days.

APPLICATIONS

The development and purpose of the mobile applications developed by ISIS indicate that its cyber capabilities may be increasing more rapidly than some security researchers believe. In 2014, ISIS released the "Dawn of Glad Tidings" application to propagate their message on Twitter, recruit new followers, and increase their renown. Thousands of users downloaded the application from Google Play store before it was removed for violating Google's community guidelines. More significantly, the application asked to access a surprising amount of personal information on the native devices, and thousands of Android users accepted those terms. Unbeknownst to them, is what ISIS, the terrorist organization, does with the data accessed. Some have alleged that the application led to identity theft, while others dismiss the claims. If ISIS goes to the trouble of developing an application and programming it to collect specific personal information, there is likely an ulterior motive. If true, then ISIS has displayed a level of sophistication, the theft and exploitation of personal identifiable information, above what it had previously. ISIS has released a few Android applications since then and it seems just as unlikely that they were created out of goodwill.

In December 2015, IBTimes and members of Anonymous reported that the ISIS Android application known as Amaq Agency might have been behind a targeted DDoS attack against the root name servers that support the global internet. The attack occurred between November 30, 2015 and December 1, 2015 and it targeted 13 internet root name servers.

In an interview with IBTimes, John McAfee claimed, "This is as serious as it gets. We have absolutely no defenses in place to counter this threat. If the perpetrators had activated more phones we would have lost the internet." Supposedly, when the application was running, it stored the addresses of the 13 root name servers in an encrypted packet, in memory. The addresses did not appear inside the static code for the application; the encrypted packet was only accessible when the application was running. The packet decrypted at runtime, which caused security researchers to wonder what contents it held. The attacks flooded the servers with a peak of 5 million queries per second. It is estimated that as few as 18,000 devices on Wi-Fi networks could have generated that volume of traffic. DEFCON organizer Eddie Mize told IBTimes, "Imagine if the internet went down for several days, I believe we would see significant power grid failure and potentially loss of emergency services. This could mean the failure of dams and flood controls, power and water distribution, natural gas distribution and control failure, and more. Perhaps the most alarming aspect would be to the financial sector. I believe that loss of the internet for even a two week period could cause enough disruption to financial institutions that consumers would lose confidence and this could be catastrophic to the markets. All of this could set up a chain reaction that could send the public in to a panicked tailspin." There are 370 more permanent servers, but taking these servers down through a similar DDoS attack would be trivial. At the peak of the DDoS attack, the servers received more than five million queries per second, and more than 50 billion queries in total during the two-day period. Verisign, whose servers were among the targets, contends that the source addresses were spoofed and therefore attribution is inconclusive.

However, the originating IPv4 addresses were evenly distributed and every request asked to resolve to the same address, which is unlikely in the event of spoofing. A targeted botnet is a more likely source of the attack. The attack was the third time since 2012 that a DDoS attack had been carried out against the root name servers. In March 2013, a group that had previously conducted DDoS attacks against Spamhaus, a spam prevention organization, attacked critical hubs for the internet relied upon by western infrastructure, such as the London Internet Exchange (LINX), the Amsterdam Internet Exchange (AMS-IX), the Frankfurt Internet Exchange (DE-CIX), and the Hong Kong Internet Exchange (HKIX).

Though an extreme scenario, the threat posed by a prolonged attack on the internet should not be underestimated. The internet was not designed with security in mind. Even with commercial tools in place to ensure some semblance of security, the underlying infrastructure supporting the internet has inherent vulnerabilities that cannot be patched or repaired. Assuming that added applications and tools can adequately secure the internet is akin to sealing the door to a house to prevent water from reaching its basement when water is already creeping through the foundation. Consider that the western internet infrastructure has approximately 60 Tbps of available bandwidth. According to Cloudfare CEO Matthew Prince, at the 2013 Defcon Conference in Las Vegas, an unsophisticated attack of 12 Tbps was very possible. An attack that drew a fifth of the available bandwidth of the western internet would disrupt business communications, traffic lights, some transportation networks, and some operations within critical infrastructure such as at water treatment plants or power generation and distribution facilities.

If such a botnet were to be fully deployed, the global impact would be "catastrophic" for financial and essential services. Mize believes "we have no defenses [against a mobile app botnet] and it was entirely unanticipated. The people in power need to be woken up before the world as we know comes to an end." Even if Verisign is correct and the attack was not the machinations of ISIS, it is important to consider the alternative.

It remains unclear how many users downloaded the Amaq Agency application because ISIS distributes the free download on Pastebin and other channels instead of through the Google Play store. In any case, cell phones are cheap. An AT&T GoPhone with Wi-Fi capabilities costs as little as $20. If ISIS deployed an infected mobile application on the mobile phone of every one of its members, then it could repeat this attack. With more than one phone per member, the results would be more significant. Consider instead, if ISIS released a mobile application that did not promote ISIS and did not appear malicious. For example, if ISIS released a "Candy-Crush knockoff" application, put it on the Google Play store for free, and conducted widespread attacks through the botted mobile devices, how many systems would be at their disposal? How much personal information would mobile gamers nonchalantly give away when they accepted the terms and conditions? Loss of the internet would harm the Western nations more than the territories controlled by ISIS. Even if the target of the DDoS were not the root name servers supporting the internet, a DDoS from a widespread number of mobile devices would be powerful.

Finally, In May 2016, the ISIS help desk developed and released an Android application called Huroof, through an active Telegram channel. Huroof is meant to teach children the Arabic alphabet through militaristic vocabulary words. It also contains Jihadist themed, flash cards, songs and cartoon animations. The application indicates that ISIS plans to sustain its occupation long enough for a new generation of militants to mature. In that case, what prevents them from tailoring their content for the younger generation towards the acquisition of information security and other technical skills? A more educated wave of jihadists will inevitably mean that the zealous organization will be more dangerous.

Mobile applications enable ISIS to quietly aggregate a store of personal information and to position insider threats to an organization. Perhaps the infected device will knowingly be carried into an organization to infect their BYOD devices on their network. Perhaps the insider threat will never realize that the game that they downloaded is spreading malware in the background. In either case, ISIS can use its budding cyber capabilities and its mobile applications to increase its reach and influence. Even if a malicious application just sent an extremist text to the user's contacts, it would still achieve a desirable impact for the terror organization.

POTENTIAL FOR THE ESCALATION OF CYBER CAPABILITIES

In April 2016, the U.S. Defense Secretary Ashton Carter gave Cyber Command its first wartime assignment. The United States publically declared its first ever cyber warfare campaign, against ISIS. The U.S. intends to use its arsenal of digital tools to disrupt and sever ISIS's communication infrastructure, and its access to money and trade. Carter hopes that cyber warfare disrupts "their ability to command their forces, interrupting their ability to plot", and hampers "their finances, their ability to pay people." In fact, many Syrian recruits, who joined ISIS to escape Syria's 57.7% unemployment rate, have recently defected due to the loss of the $400-1200 monthly wage (determined by number of dependents). These members initially joined because the Syrian army salary starts at $63 per month and its opposition, the FSA pays fighters $36 per month. Directing Cyber Command against ISIS will expand the military's reach without sending more troops into the region. Carter agrees, stating, "We are thinking more strategically about shifting our response-planning from fighting a war to also providing decision makers with options to deter and forestall a conflict before it begins." The media refers to these cyber-attacks as "cyber bombs"; however, that term is wrought with ambiguity and elevated expectations. The cyber-attacks that the United States conducts against adversarial systems are not point-and-fire missiles or cataclysmic devices. In many cases, the "cyber-bombs" that the American government is using against ISIS and other targets consist of a layered combination of basic off-the-shelf commercial products and advanced proprietary (and often classified) systems made for the exclusive use of our defense, intelligence, and law enforcement communities. More frequently, a "cyber-bomb" or "cyber-weapon" refers to a collection of hardware and software and the knowledge of their potential uses against a given target. In most instances, unlike with a bomb, our cyber forces do not want the enemy to be aware that their system is compromised. That means no catastrophic fallout and no flashy delivery. The efforts against ISIS likely begin with distributed denial of service (DDoS) attacks to overload the adversary's servers with a large amount of traffic to prevent legitimate use. When ISIS cannot access its servers or systems, it has a more difficult time communicating, deploying resources, and recruiting. The United States has also began conducting a counter propaganda campaign focused on the promotion of voices in the region on social media to dispute ISIS lies and deceptive claims on social media.

There are now five times as many anti-ISIS channels on social media as proponents. By undermining the fundamentalist message, recruitment into the group plummets and additional resources must be applied to draw in a steady influx of fresh recruits. The campaign causes locals and potential recruits to see alternatives to terrorism, such as faith in the democratic process, as rewarding. Further, defeating ISIS's messaging machine on the cyber battlefield discourages other groups like Al Qaeda, Al Shabaab, and Boko Haram from further developing their cyber capabilities. As a result of the campaign, ISIS recruitment accounts have demonstratively fewer followers and tweet less frequently than in the past. The jihadists have also had to migrate to different, less trafficked platforms such as Telegram and secure messengers to convey their propaganda undisturbed. Some followers have even left ISIS due to an awakened disillusionment with its ideology and discriminatory practices in the organization. ISIS pays Syrian members far less than it pays European or Gulf militants. Some campaigns remind recruits that the organizational beliefs are un-Islamic and inhuman, and hypocritical. Further, some members are abandoning the cause because they are convinced that it is losing.

Military strategic cyber-attacks are not simple endeavors. Technological experts, military strategists, researchers, political analysts, lawyers, and military experts are required for such a campaign to develop tools and tactics and to ensure that the strategy aligns with national interests, follows national and international laws and treaties, and addresses the threat. Intelligence and counterterrorism efforts, led by the NSA or GCHQ for example, might routinely collect real names, user ids, network addresses, IP addresses, online chat logs, and other data from across the internet using classified and unclassified methods, in order to establish interconnections and inferences about potentially alarming online activity. Afterward, specific threat actors can then be monitored in greater detail. The agency can use the information to arrest suspects, issue fake instructions to militants, or otherwise disrupt malicious activities. Cyber-attacks against critical infrastructure must be planned and coordinated. The aforementioned intelligence efforts can identify and monitor these campaigns before any harm is realized. However, the increasing ubiquity of anonymization and secure communication mechanisms among malcontents may severely hamper law enforcement's attempts to preclude incidents. Consequently, it is imperative that intelligence efforts remain vigilant on the latest tools, tactics, procedures, applications, and channels. A strategy of creating backdoors in secure applications for the purpose of monitoring potential activity will not work because adversaries avoid those channels and it would have catastrophic impacts on national security because adversaries would figure out how to exploit the vulnerability intentionally introduced in the applications. The only solution is to remain technologically more advanced than the adversary.

In some instances, advanced cyber-attacks may include customized software created to limit adversarial activity. Consider the Stuxnet malware that the United States and Israel allegedly used against Iranian nuclear facilities in April 2010. Stuxnet targeted Siemens industrial control systems (ICS) in developing nations such as Iran (~59%), Indonesia (~18%), and India (~8%). It contained a programmable logic controller (PLC) rootkit designed to spy upon, subvert, and in some cases sabotage Siemens supervisory control and data acquisition (SCADA) systems that regulated specific industrial systems. Stuxnet caused the centrifuges used in the Iranian uranium enrichment facilities, equipment in the oil production facilities and other critical infrastructure systems to operate differently than intended without revealing the errors to the user. ICIT Fellow John Miller (Cylance) noted, "While the capabilities to attack and affect critical infrastructure first came to public light during the Stuxnet attack on Iran in 2010, we have yet to encounter a serious attack on US infrastructure. The reason we have yet to encounter a serious CI attack has to do with offensive cyber-capabilities being primarily possessed by nation state actors, allowing federal authorities the ability to attribute a hack back to an attacking country and provide a proportional response, essentially ensuring mutual destruction." Cyber-terrorists are less concerned with retaliatory cyberattacks than nation states because the terrorist have less critical infrastructure under their control. Their main limitation at the moment is a lack of technical personnel and a lack of sophisticated malware.

It is possible that the United States or one of its allies are employing similar, though likely much more sophisticated, malware against the refinery systems under ISIS control. It is equally likely that Russia, whose nation state APT groups focus on espionage, and who has launched cyber-physical warfare in the past, has deployed malware against ISIS. Both nations must remain cautious and premediate their actions with extreme care to prevent ISIS from developing new, dangerous capabilities. At the very least, increased cyber- pressure could cause the group to move deeper into secure messaging channels or it could cause them to invest significant funds into developing offensive cyber capabilities for retaliation. Worse, ISIS could discover the malware and dedicate resources to reverse engineering the code so that it could use the malware on other targets. How much harm could ISIS cause if it acquired a copy of the newest variant of the BlackEnergy malware?

On December 23, 2015, a Sandworm campaign against the Prykarpattyaoblenegro power plant in Ukraine caused a severe outage. More significant than the immediate loss of power, the threat actor, demonstrated that the malware, which can be purchased on the dark web, can severely cripple a nation's critical infrastructure as part of a cyber-physical campaign

The BlackEnergy malware is available for purchase in cyber underground communities. The BlackEnergy toolkit features a builder application that generates the clients used to infect victim systems, it features server-side scripts to create C&C servers, and it includes an interface for the attacker to communicate with their botnet. F-Secure comments that the toolkit is simple enough and convenient enough that anyone can build a botnet without possessing extensive technical skills. If ISIS has hackers of remotely the same skill level as "TriCk", then they likely could operate a copy of BlackEnergy

The BlackEnergy malware originally appeared around 2007 as a tool to create botnets for distributed denial of service (DDoS) attacks. Plugins enabled the malware to be used to send spam emails or steal bank credentials.

The most notorious application of the malware was its use in cyberattacks against Georgia during the Russo-Georgian conflict in 2008.

Since then, criminals and advanced persistent threat actors have upgraded the malware at least twice. No matter the version, BlackEnergy has a vast capability to disrupt the availability of victim systems. Stuxnet, the malware to which BlackEnergy is most often compared, required unique knowledge of the specific target domain and environment.

BlackEnergy requires no such knowledge to operate. The malware is simple and becoming increasingly easier to use as new variants are developed and disseminated.

The BlackEnergy toolkit contains a builder application that can be used to generate the clients that attackers use to infect victim systems. Server-side scripts in the toolkit can be used to set up command and control servers and to provide an interface for control of the bots. The simplicity and convenience of the toolkit allow anyone possessing the kit to build a botnet without any technical skills.

Figure 1: BlackEnergy (2007) Builder

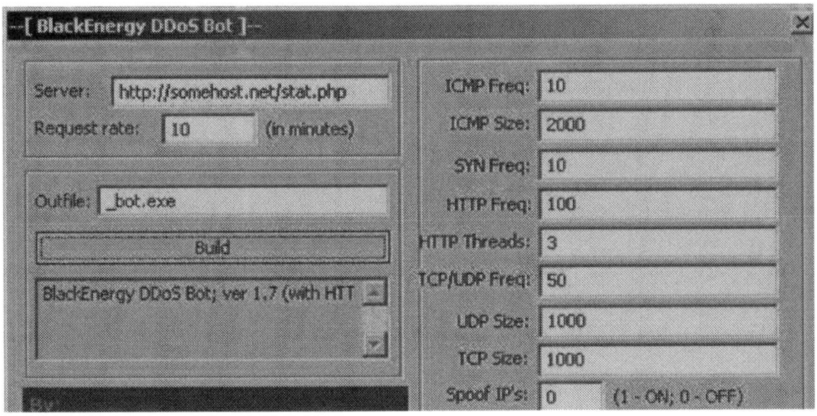

Source: F-Secure BlackEnergy & Quedagh: The Convergence of Crimeware and APT Attacks

Around 2010, malicious threat actors rewrote the code for BlackEnergy according to a more professional development cycle. This second iteration was designed for simple use and scalability. It included a rudimentary installer and a modular structure. In 2011, the framework was updated with User Access Control (UAC) bypass installers to enable the malware to acquire elevated code execution privileges through the framework that Microsoft developed to enable legacy applications to work with newer versions of Windows. Essentially, the malware will only infect a system if the active user is a member of the local administrator group; otherwise, the malware attempts to bypass UAC by either relaunching itself as Administrator on Vista or by exploiting a backwards compatibility feature in later versions of Windows. In 2013, the second version of the malware was updated with 64-bit driver support.

In mid-2014, the third variant of BlackEnergy was discovered. As with the second version, malicious actors rewrote the BlackeEnergy code to include more advanced features and a simpler and more efficient development structure. Due to its diverse and powerful set of plugins, BlackEnergy 3 is a powerful tool for cybercriminals and state-sponsored threat actors. Some researchers believe that this more advanced version was developed by a sophisticated state-sponsored group in an attempt to obscure their activity amongst the activity of numerous cybercriminals.

BlackEnergy 3 does not contain a driver, it uses a timestamp for its build ID, and it includes many sophisticated plugins. Its plugins are designed to prevent deconstruction of the malware in virtual environments, defend the malware against anti-debugging techniques, and kill the program if specific security features or countermeasures are detected. The plugins include: a parasitic infector, system information for the malware, a remote desktop client and the ability to view the screen of the infected host, the ability to scan the networks connected to the victim, an update mechanism for the malware, and a module to "destroy" the victim system. The malware also includes the ability: to enumerate file systems, to log keystrokes, to capture stored passwords, to take screenshots, to discover networks and remotely execute, to list Windows accounts, and to query system hardware, BIOS and Windows info. The malware also contains a wiper component, Kill-Disk, that removes the malware, and potentially all stored data, from the system. Some distributions of BlackEnergy 3 contain fake Microsoft digital certificates. Signed digital certificates are used to authenticate software code and indicate that the code has not been altered or corrupted. The fake certificates reduce trust in the system and suggest development by a sophisticated threat group.

In March 2015, multiple Ukrainian state institutions received a spear-phishing email allegedly from the Supreme Council of Ukraine. The email contained a malicious XLS attachment with a macro in it. If the document was opened, then the macro executed, and it created a dropper for either BlackEnergy 2 or BlackEnergy 3. Once the attackers infected a network, they compromised a web server and established a beachhead for a persistent presence. The establishment and maintenance of the beachhead relied on freely available tools for creating web shells, for tunneling, and for SSH servers. The spear phishing emails contained a SMTP header that pointed to the IP address and the name of the mail server used to launch the campaign. The attacks in December 2015 followed the same attack chain, except the malicious attachment in the spear-phishing email was an Excel spreadsheet. The SMTP header matched that of the previous attacks and the energy sector was a target in both campaigns.

In December 2015, BlackEnergy 3 was deployed against the Prykarpattya Oblenergo and Kyivoblenergo energy facilities in the Ukraine. Trend Micro also reports that the malware was deployed against mining and rail facilities as part of the same campaign. All of the samples exhibited the same functionality and they communicated with the same command and control (C2) server. The attacks coincided with Russian military activity in the region. While security firms such as F-Secure have attributed the activity to the Quedagh (aka Sandworm) group, the attribution is not definitive. This group, which may be sponsored by the Russian government, conducts politically-oriented attacks. Though the malware might have been developed by Quedagh, it is currently being used and distributed by multiple criminal and espionage groups. It is possible that Quedagh sells its service to the state sponsor and is otherwise free to sell its malware or conduct other operations. It is also possible that malware was obtained from an infection or compromised server and distributed. In either case, the developer may have allowed the spread of the malware to complicate attribution attempts.

One theory of the December 2015 campaign is that the malware was intended to destabilize Ukraine by massive and persistent disruption of its power, mining, and transport infrastructure. Another possibility is that the adversaries deployed the malware against numerous critical infrastructure systems in order to identify which ones were the most susceptible to infection. It is also possible that the actors were just testing the capabilities of the malware before selling it or deploying it elsewhere.

The BlackEnergy malware does not solely target SCADA systems. It threatens systems and organizations in all sectors – public and private. The first two versions of BlackEnergy were used to steal confidential information. In the 2015 attacks, BlackEnergy 3 also disrupted the operation of the Ukrainian power grid. Unlike Stuxnet, the malware is simple to use and easy to acquire and modify.

ISIS could use the BlackEnergy malware to conduct disruptive attacks on ICS or SCADA systems, and thereby disrupt critical services in target regions. Moreover, the malware has a significant impact on affected systems, is easy to operate, and is available for purchase in certain forums of the dark web. If motivated to acquire the malware through opposition or other pressure, ISIS could easily launch a devastating attack while also conducting physical attacks or while layering other cyber components into the campaigns.

POTENTIAL CAPABILITIES

ISIS already teaches its militants about encryption in the manuals that it distributes from the "help desk" and in publications like Kybernetiq. Assuming that parts or all of ISIS want to increase available funds, inflict financial harm on "Crusaders", and disrupt critical operation in Western nations, with the least amount of prerequisite technical knowledge and monetary investment, then it is surprising that the Cyber Caliphate has not already popularized ransomware attacks within the organization. Ransomware is a form of malware that weaponizes encryption to prevent the victim from accessing their systems or data until a payment has been made to the attacker and the files have been unlocked using a decryption key.

Ransomware can also be used to lock down a target system for a time, or as one stage of a layered attack that involves distracting the user with ransomware while the files on the system are searched and exfiltrated. Ransomware made a large resurgence in February 2016 when medical systems belonging to Hollywood Presbyterian Medical Center were infected with the Locky ransomware. After nearly two weeks of stunted operations, the hospital paid a $17,000 ransom. Almost overnight, adversaries began developing and distributing new variants of ransomware that charged users hundreds or thousands of dollars to free their systems.

Ransomware is a favorite among the unsophisticated hacking communities because it is easy to distribute, has a high return on investment, and it can be purchased as a Ransomware-as-a-Service (RaaS) model. Under the RaaS model, a sophisticated adversary writes the malware and then sells or distributes it to numerous less skilled hackers, who then distribute it to victims. If the victims pay the ransom, then the malware developer receives a percentage of the ransom. Ransomware and RaaS are easily purchased on online forums; as a result, terrorist groups such as ISIS would not have any difficult purchasing a variant on the dark net or working under a RaaS model. While Locky is currently the most popular and most abundant ransomware variant, ISIS would likely benefit more from the Cerber ransomware.

The Cerber ransomware began to infect systems in late February 2016 by encrypting their files with AES encryption until a ransom of 1.24 Bitcoins (~$500) was transferred to the attackers. The ransomware is available for purchase or as a RaaS on closed Russian markets on the dark web. The former option means that a group, like ISIS, could train personnel, purchase a copy, duplicate it for any number of cyber-trained operatives, and conduct attacks for financial gain, to disrupt services, or to incite fear or panic. The latter option enables the operatives to deliver the malware and conduct attacks through simplified graphical user interfaces on the condition that the Cerber developers earn a commission of each ransom payment.

Ransomware, like Cerber, can be delivered through phishing emails, transferred through watering-hole attacks, or distributed through botnets. Malwarebytes discovered that Cerber is also delivered via the Magnitude exploit kit through malvertising networks on adult, torrent, and streaming websites. The campaign leverages a vulnerability in Internet Explorer to fingerprint possible victims to ensure that only genuine systems are infected. The fingerprinting process includes enumeration of the local file system, detection of virtual machines, detection of certain security software, and detection of web debuggers. FireEye reported that the malware was similarly delivered through the Nuclear Pack zero- day Flash exploit. If no software to detect the malware is detected, then the malvertising landing page infects the victim system. FireEye also observed the ransomware delivered through the same macro downloader spam distribution framework used by the Dridex criminal group. In this model, the victim receives an email with a malicious attachment that contains a macro that drops the VBScript in the %appdate% path of the system. The VBScript contains obfuscated code that is used to download the Cerber payload. VBScript checks for internet connectivity, and if internet is available, it sends an HTTP Range Request to fetch a JPEG file from a malicious URL. A value in the Range header indicates to the attacker's web server to only return content beginning at a predetermined offset of the JPG file. The response content of this request is XORed with a key and decrypted as the Cerber payload. The variant has also been detected in emails, in Word files and in Steam gaming related files. In some cases, attackers bypass spam filters by using double zipped Windows Script Files (WSF) in malicious emails to deliver the malware.

Upon execution, Cerber checks whether the victim's system is located in a former Soviet state; if so, then the malware automatically terminates. Cyber-Jihadists would have to either remove this stipulation by editing the JSON file or focus their campaign on Western nations. If it executes, then Cerber installs itself in the %AppData%\{2ED2A2FE-872C- D4A0-17AC-E301404F1CBA}\ folder and names itself after a random Windows executable. It then executes a command to configure Windows to boot into Safe Mode with Networking on the next reboot. It also configures itself to start automatically when the victim logs into Windows, to set itself as the screensaver if the system goes idle, and to execute itself as a task every minute. The ransomware then issues fake system alerts until the system is allowed to restart. The system will reboot into Safe Mode with Networking, shutdown again after the user logs in, and then reboot into normal mode. Once the user logs in, Cerber begins encrypting the victim's files with AES-256 bit encryption. A JSON configuration file, included with the malware, details what extensions and files to encrypt, what countries to not infect, and other configuration information. Encrypted files are appended with the

.CERBER extension. Cerber contains the ability to scan for, enumerate, and infect Windows files shares and networked drives. The ransomware creates three ransom notes (a .txt,

.html, and .vbs file) on the victim desktop and in every folder containing encrypted files. The ransom note contains instructions to access Tor, purchase Bitcoins, and an address to pay the ransom.

The .vbs files contain a VBScript that causes the victim machine to verbally inform the victim of the infection by repeating a message from the attacker. Traditionally, the vocal reminder that files are encrypted jars victims and pressures them into making the irrational decision to pay the ransom. A Cyber-Jihadist group could alter the message to spew propaganda in order to incite panic, increase notoriety, or otherwise harass the victim. The audio message continues to repeat until the victim either pays the ransom or removes all of the VBS files from the system.

Figure 2: Cerber VBS Script

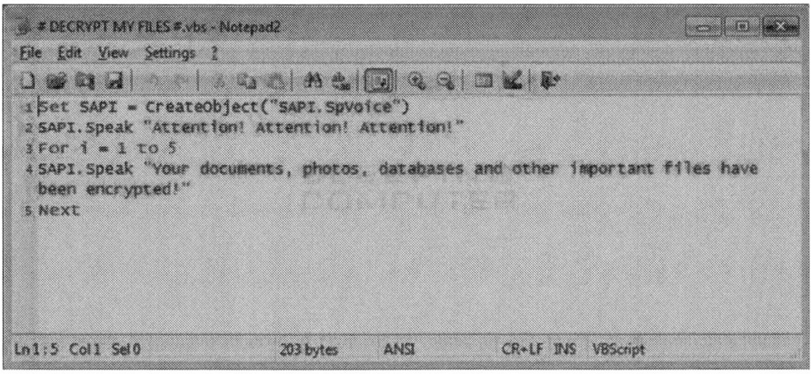

Source: http://www.bleepingcomputer.com/news/security/the-cerber-ran-somware-not-only-encrypts- your-data-but-also-speaks-to-you/

The site to pay the Cerber ransom is available in 12 different languages. The ransom is doubled if the victim does not pay within 7 days. When the attackers receive the entire payment, the interface provides the victim with a decryptor tool unique to their system. At the time of this writing, there is no way to recover the files encrypted by Cerber ransomware without the decryptor tool.

Whether or not the files are decrypted after payment is sent is dependent upon the attacker. Though some criminals decline to decrypt files after payment is received, many traditional cyber criminals often decrypt the victim files because the ransomware business model only remains profitable if victims believe that they can get their files back by paying the demanded Bitcoins. If every attacker left the files encrypted, then the attack vector would be notorious as a scam and no victim would ever pay. Groups, such as ISIS, benefit from the disruption and chaos of permanently encrypting the files on a target system almost as much as they benefit from the ransom itself. Further, if the group employs ransomware as a diversionary tactic or as part of a layered attack, then it is in their best interest not to decrypt the files. While the victim is responding to the attack or reverting their files from a backup, the terrorists or their hired mercenaries could exfiltrate data relevant to future attacks, steal PII or electronic health information (EHI) to sell or use, or launch a cyber-physical attack.

In March 2016, Cerber was modified to also turn infected systems into bots for DDoS attacks. The additional functionality is likely a secondary source of revenue in case the victim does not pay the ransom. Victim machines are used to flood the subnet with UDP packets over port 6892. By spoofing the source address, a collection of bots can be used to render a target unresponsive by flooding the system with traffic. The attackers use Visual Basic to launch a file-less attack, which most anti-virus and security applications do not preemptively block. The scanners do not detect the attack until files are dropped on disk, after the attack has succeeded. The botnet may be directed against other victims, against targets of opportunity, or they may be rented out on the Dark Web.

EVOLUTION OF THE THREAT

Cyber-terrorist groups, such as the UCC face extraordinary opposition from organizations, government entities, and other hacking groups. Twitter, Facebook, and many other social media and messaging services actively takedown recruitment pages or work with intelligence agencies to disrupt operations or locate members. Governments dedicate resources such as personnel, computing power, funds, and even sophisticated Advanced Persistent Threat (APT) groups to crippling jihadist critical infrastructure such as communication channels, intangible assets, or monetary transfers. Opposing hacker collectives, such as Anonymous, take down social media accounts, expose members, and otherwise hamper operations. So far, ISIS has responded to its resounding digital opposition by increasing its cyber defensive capabilities and its operational security.

However, as efforts to hamper its operations escalate, such as the United States declaration of Cyber-War on ISIS or the sudden decrease of available funds within the organization that resulted from recent airstrikes, the militant group will be forced to adapt under pressure. It could fracture into decentralized factions, or it might rapidly develop new capabilities in retaliation. Though the loss of funds resulting in some alleged internal strife within ISIS, the group is known among terror organizations for having a surprisingly resilient structure. In the event that factions form, it is possible that one of the subgroups will develop cyber offensive capabilities to acquire funds and increase its notoriety and influence. ICIT Fellow Danyetta Magana (Covenant Security Solutions) explains, "It is a fallacy that extremist groups are not computer smart, in fact to the opposite. As history repeats itself over and over again, all armies have gone from bow and arrows to cannons, from cannons to machines guns, and to ballistic missiles and fighter jets in the air. This is referred to as a revolution of military affairs across all domains. Being able to overcome your adversaries offensive and defense is simply the art of war, and the same holds true for the cyber domain." The increased pressure on ISIS could cause members to seek new weapons to level the playing field.

Under the tutelage of Junaid Hussain, ISIS developed a wide proficiency on a diverse collection of secure messaging applications, social media, and anonymity tools. Usage of these tools as well as operational security measures fueled by paranoia, were propagated to ISIS members through their publications, recruitment manuals, and internal communications. The adoption of these cyber capabilities confounded counterintelligence efforts to monitor communications and analyze signal intelligence. The increasing opposition to ISIS has pushed them into using more obscure, more secure communication applications (such as Wickr instead of WhatsApp), and has caused them to retreat further into the unindexed portions of the internet known as the dark net or deep web. ISIS members are familiar with encryption techniques, anonymity methods, online tracking mechanisms such as cookies, tokens, and beacons, and other information security topics. This basic knowledge means that the extremists can understand how to conduct attacks, how to use basic malware, and how to deploy ransomware, even without sophisticated technical capabilities. The group understands the necessity of using cheap or disposable devices and of remaining paranoid as a matter of operational security. While digital opposition to the group was necessary, it had the adverse effect of instigating an internal education initiative that taught members to use the exact tools, techniques, and procedures that can enable them to rapidly acquire cyber-offensive capabilities. Black Hat security professionals pander their wares and services on deep web markets and forums. These hackers communicate with one another using many of the applications already familiar to ISIS members. Given ISIS's diverse membership, they are unimpeded by language barriers that might limit the browsing and purchasing power of other groups. The adoption of anonymous currencies such as Bitcoins enables the group to transfer assets across the globe to members or sellers, in a matter of seconds, with near absolute anonymity. In fact, some online personas claiming affiliation with the Islamic State have already attempted to illicit Bitcoin donations for ISIS from social media users. Another supporter released a guide detailing how to donate Bitcoins and support ISIS, along with the benefits of digital currencies. The author, who assumes the name "Taqi'ulDeen al-Munthir," argues that digital currencies such as Bitcoin are the best option for militant jihadist organizations because adoption frees them of reliance on a currency backed by the global market or an enemy nation state. He continues that anonymous currencies allow foreign supporters to donate to ISIS even though banks and financial institutions will not allow the transfer of funds to the group. The author suggests the formation of Bitcoin backed "Shari' only" markets that transcend all borders and nation state regulations. The adoption of anonymous currency could hasten ISIS's ability to hire hackers or purchase complex exploit kits.

Even in its current state, ISIS already has the resources and capability to recruit or hire sophisticated cyber-professionals on the dark web. It is possible, and even probable, that ISIS has already been purchasing attacks on Western organizations and critical infrastructure for years. Groups like ISIS might hate Western culture and practices, but they have no qualms about appropriating and weaponizing material and assets developed in those regions. They use guns manufactured in the United States and Russia and vehicles from Japan, so why would they refuse to use malware or hackers from foreign nations. To the zealots, the cyber assets are just more weapons to use in their battle. In all likelihood, the cyber-mercenaries hired would not know if they were conducting attacks on behalf of the terrorist organization. As a result of the anonymity that the hackers themselves rely on, they would unknowingly infect systems, steal data, or otherwise cause chaos for a terror organization. Given a fiscal asset portfolio at a very conservative estimate of over $1 billion, ISIS can hire many hackers to conduct many attacks. If those attacks result in stolen data, intellectual property, or other intangible assets, then the organization can sell the data to perpetuate the cycle.

ICIT Fellow Malcolm Harkins (Cylance) adds, "While Cyber-Jihadists will undoubtedly be driven to exploit vulnerabilities in our industrial control systems to inflict physical harm on our nation, terrorist organizations have already used cybercrime to raise millions of dollars to fund 'traditional' attacks like the 2008 bombings in Mumbai. As Cyber-Jihadism grows, it is safe to assume that we will most likely see a spike in both physical and digital attacks from these groups." ISIS may lack the ability to conduct sophisticated cyber-attacks without help, but it has exceptional operational planning capabilities. It can conduct large, sophisticated cyber-attacks against critical infrastructure systems or organizations by compartmentalizing the stages of the attack and hiring different hackers to conduct different layers of the overall attack. By doing so, ISIS increases the likelihood of remaining anonymous and it increases the likelihood that the attack will succeed along at least one vector. Some sophisticated collectives, such as Carbanak, may even be willing to conduct the entire attack with a guarantee of success, for a high enough reward. If ISIS acquires cyber-capable personnel, it can realize equivalent success by outsourcing components of an attack toolkit and then combining the tools into a more formidable asset.

Cyber-terrorist groups can use layered attacks to devastating effects. For instance, a group could hire a hacker to cause chaos in a city by disrupting its traffic system or water flow or it could conduct a physical attack to inflict losses and incite panic. After emergency services were burdened with casualties and the injured, the terrorists could launch DDoS and ransomware attacks against hospital and emergency response services. The extremists could use malware to steal confidential information from the infected systems while law enforcement attempted to respond to the attacks. Next, attacks against the SCADA and ICS systems supporting the local electric grid could further plunge the target city into turmoil. Finally, physical militants could invade the city and utilize the sense of panic and burden to overwhelm its defenses. After the city was conquered, the group, or its hired help, could cease the attacks. Through this basic and possible scenario, the group could capture entire regions without destroying the underlying infrastructure.

3 | OPPORTUNITY

INSIDER THREAT

ISIS can use recruitment infrastructure and any PII or EHI collected from attacks, to recruit and place insider threats at organizations and government agencies. Not all ISIS recruits are the stereotypical Middle Eastern men. They have also recruited Caucasian teenagers from Wisconsin and African American adults from Minnesota. ISIS keeps meticulous records and all new recruits must complete a data sheet recording their entry date, nationality, blood type, date of birth, education level, and former employment. According to 4000 records leaked to journalists by defectors, 63.3% of recruits originate in the Middle East or North Africa, 15.7% came from countries near the Middle East including Russia, 10.6% originated in Europe, 3.4% were from Asia, and 1.15% were from the Americas or Australia. ISIS lures in troubled and lonely individuals and slowly persuades them to adopt its ideology by engendering a sense of purpose and community in their minds. Of those 4000 recruits, 87.4% were born between 1980 and 1999, with an average birth year of 1988. Outside of science fiction, there is no way to know what ideology an individual cherishes in their mind. Insider threats might install backdoors or malware on networks as part of layered attacks or they might collect information about operations, systems, or facilities to enable the extremist group to conduct cyber, physical, or cyber-physical attacks. Unlike the initial ISIS fighters, the new recruits are educated enough to fill positions in organizations. The leaked data reveals that 61.2% of the militants had at least a high school education and 29.2% had at least one semester of post high school education.

Approximately 15.6% of the sample batch was current college students. Students open their minds to new avenues of thought and perception when they attend college. They are also the primary users of social media. Consequently, college students are extremely vulnerable and extremely valuable recruits for jihadist organizations such as ISIS, who are desperate for educated recruits to fill technical positions within the organization. Any number of the militant recruits, who abandoned their studies to join ISIS could be sent back to school to finish their degrees, to recruit other students, or to graduate and infiltrate organizations and government entities.

In early May 2016, the Islamic State Hacking Division released a tweet claiming, "In our next leak we may even disclose secret intelligence the Islamic State has just received from a source the brothers in the UK have spent some time acquiring from the Ministry of Defence in London as we slowly and secretly infiltrate England and the USA online and off." Law enforcement authorities did not comment on the authenticity of the claim. Since past information releases have been gathered from publically available information, there is some inherent doubt to the claim. Nevertheless, the potential for insider threats within organizations must be treated as a serious threat before it actually happens. According to the "IBM 2015 Cyber Security Intelligence Index," 45% of attacks are the result of the actions of threat actors who are external to the network, malicious insider carry out 31.5% of all attacks and 23.5% of attacks occur due to mistakes of inadvertent threat actors, who are also categorized as insider threats.

Social media, personnel devices, cloud applications, mobility and big data are making insider threats harder to identify while also providing more ways to pass protected information. Insider threats can often be categorized as: disgruntled employees who leave the company but retain access to old privileges or create back doors before leaving; malicious insiders taking advantage of expired or orphan accounts to attack valuable resources or with privileged access who sell information for financial gain; and the inadvertent insiders who do not mean harm but fall prey to social engineering schemes that grant access to outside attackers. Trusted third-party contract workers may be "quasi- insiders" if their actions or inaction results in an inadvertent breach of the network or in the breach of a supporting network.

Cyber-Jihadist organizations heavily recruit "troubled individuals," such as disgruntled employees, social outcasts, and misguided youths. Further, they have the capital to entice resentful personnel to sell data or commit actions that compromise the integrity of the network. Unlike nation-state intelligence and counter intelligence entities, ISIS, and similar organizations, assumes immense risk every time they contact a potential recruit; as a result, they are more adapt at perceiving the disposition and needs of a target and at organically convincing that individual to bend to their will. What would an employee at a supporting organization like an HVAC or a background check firm do for a sizable paycheck if they felt malice towards their employer and they were offered an untraceable fortune of Bitcoins? Would they plug in a USB? Would they intentionally click a phishing email? The OPM breach may have also been the result of the compromise of supporting organizations. Hacking into intelligence databases or remote controlling military drones is currently outside the capabilities of Cyber-Jihadists because they lack the sophisticated tools, techniques, and procedures to bypass sophisticated security mechanisms; however, if they can compromise tangential networks, then they can laterally move onto those networks and establish a persistent presence. Essentially, terrorist organizations can compensate for their lack of cyber capabilities by exploiting vulnerable humans within the organizational network.

MEDIA

Jihadist groups regularly deface websites and blogs belonging to media outlets because traffic is already directed towards their websites, channels, and publications. In the future, media outlets may experience more compromising attacks from extremist organizations who desire advance knowledge of breaking stories, confidential sources, and internal information about public figures. ISIS in particular believes that every journalist is a spy; consequently, they are known for executing media personalities in the region.

In April 2015, the Cyber Caliphate supposedly attacked the French media outlet Tv5 Monde. The attack resulted in temporary control of the website, social media accounts, and the disruption of 11 stations for a few hours. At the same time, the group published threats to a list of names of French soldiers and family members. The attack may have been facilitated by poor cyber security practices on behalf of Tv5 Monde. Even though ISIS claimed responsibility for the attack, alternate theories suggest that the attack may have been perpetrated by the Russian APT 28 and then attributed to ISIS to cover their tracks because the Sednit malware was found on the infected systems. It is possible both APT 28, who is known to rely on the Sednit malware, and ISIS maintained a foothold in the same system and that one exploitation may have facilitated or revealed the other. It is also possible that ISIS purchased and deployed a copy of the malware.

ICS AND SCADA SYSTEMS

The ICS and SCADA systems upon which American critical infrastructure depends are antiquated and vulnerable. Systems in facilities supporting sectors ranging from energy production to nuclear defense, have recently been the focus of discussions about modernization efforts. The aforementioned Russian BlackEnergy malware can be used to compromise critical systems such as electrical grids. Variants, which are less sophisticated, are available for purchase on dark web forums. The same malware can be used to target financial and healthcare systems. Some organizations rely on their antiquated systems because they incorrectly believe that the systems are protected by the obscurity of their programming. Even if sophisticated malware cannot operate on some systems, threats remain. Any system that can process code is vulnerable to ransomware because the simple malware relies only on an encryption algorithm. Ransomware is simple to use and most variants cost less than a few thousand dollars on dark web markets. ICS and SCADA systems are renown among hackers for being easy and available targets. Hackers used to earn their first bragging rights by compromising systems belonging to a water treatment or electrical facility. Most who compromise these networks seek online recognition or fiscal reward. ICIT Fellow Danyetta Magana (Covenant Security Solutions) cautions, "A Cyber- Jihad will use cyber offensive tools to adversely affect many things Americans value in everyday life and use the internet to achieve, such as running water, agriculture, highways, traffic lights, electric, postal service, gas, banks, and healthcare." Cyber-Jihadist groups may aim to disrupt operations or to overwhelm systems into shutting down or behaving abnormally. Even if the collective lacked the skills necessary to compromise a particular critical infrastructure facility, some mercenary black hats or insiders might consider the task an easy assignment for a meager financial reward. ICIT Fellow Kevin Chalker (GRA Quantum) remarks, "Today's Cyber-Jihadists are unskilled outsiders, able to accomplish little remotely from the shadows beyond temporary website defacements or service interruptions. However, if groups like ISIS could ever recruit agents working inside of critical infrastructure facilities, say power plants or water treatment facilities, our perception of the threat they pose would be catastrophically changed overnight."

In October 2015, U.S. law enforcement officials revealed that hackers tied to the Islamic State were actively attempting to breach ICS and SCADA systems in the Energy sector. Caitlin Durkovich, the assistant secretary for Infrastructure Protection at the Department of Homeland Security confirmed to company executives at a conference on American energy that," ISIL is beginning to perpetrate cyberattacks." Specific details were not provided other than that the attacks were not successful. Law enforcement also expressed concern about the growing capabilities of other domestic and foreign hate groups.

Thankfully, even successful attacks on the United States Energy Sector would not have the same impact as those against Ukraine in 2015, because the grid is much larger and minutely segmented.

FINANCIAL SECTOR

The financial sector is most vulnerable to insider threats and to poor cyber hygiene. Bank customers and employees often rely on outdated browsers, often reuse weak passwords, and often lack the training necessary to recognize phishing emails and malicious attachments. Regulators rigorously monitor banks' vulnerabilities, but undertrained personnel undermine their efforts. Extremists or mercenary hackers could easily send out phishing emails containing malware in malicious attachments to obtain personal or financial information from infected systems. Cybercrime is the largest threat to the banking sector. According to a Congressional hearing from June 2015, a major U.S. bank suffers a cyberattack every 34 seconds. According to Christopher Finan, who worked at the Pentagon on cybersecurity issues with the White House when the Nasdaq was hacked in 2010 and later served as President Barack Obama's cybersecurity adviser, in the financial sector, security systems have been applied at the end of the design process instead of at the start, resulting in a "hodgepodge of systems that have been cobbled together." Any hacker with enough time and resources can crack into the system. Stock exchanges focus on ensuring the integrity of the financial data under the assumption that hackers are bound to gain access to their system somehow. They want to make transactions indelible so that trades are intentional and validated. In response, cyber adversaries just target brokerage accounts to appear legitimate before initiating unauthorized trading. Neither cyber terrorists nor more sophisticated APT groups are capable of toppling the global stock market. To do so, an attacker would have to simultaneously hack and manipulate data in numerous separate systems. Finan comments that such an attack would have "Extraordinarily low probability but extraordinarily high consequence." Instead, threat actors can disrupt specific markets, cause chaos, harm the reputations of target organizations, and illicit financial gains by manipulating stocks and accounts of individual firms.

RESPONSE TO THE THREAT

Organizations need to act now to protect their reputation and their systems from harm before Cyber-Jihadist groups develop more sophisticated offensive capabilities. ICIT Fellow John Miller (Cylance) warns, "Regardless of proactive response, ISIS will gain the ability to attack, compromise, and disrupt national and international critical infrastructure within the next 24 months, giving them the ability to disrupt communications, utilities, and transportation in a coordinated global attack. It would require the coordinated effort of multiple attackers and a level of skill and funding that would allow access to the technologies used in critical infrastructure networks, but this could be easily overcome with under $100,000 in funding and a team smaller than the average baseball team." Organizations should begin by hiring an information security team and by conducting a risk assessment of their assets. The assessment should systematically identify potential adversaries, threats, critical assets, the short-term and the long-term impact of stolen data, how stolen data can be used, and the likelihood of different scenarios. Facilities and assets should be physically secured against insider threats and compromise. Next, the organization should patch, update, and secure its website. Pictures of the facility, online maps, and any other information that could be used to determine physical security or network infrastructure should be removed from the online profile. The information security teams that work with the organization should segment the network, protect information according to its value, and assign user access according to a principle of least necessary privilege and least access. Employees should follow a basic cyber hygiene program that includes training to recognize phishing emails and suspicious activity. The information security team should secure the network with a minimum of a firewall, IDS/ IPS systems, and antivirus/ anti-malware applications. These controls will minimize the risk of stolen user credentials and recognized malware. More sophisticated security systems, such as multifactor authentication, a User Behavior Analytics (UBA) system and a User Access Control (UAC) system, can be added to reduce the success rate and impact of insider threats. All systems and network traffic should be logged in case incidents need to be forensically investigated. All systems should be separately backed up to prevent ransomware attacks from crippling the organization. Systems should be regularly updated and patched against known threats, to prevent unsophisticated attackers from breaching the network. Organizations can further confound attackers by deploying honeypots, jump boxes, and virtual system on the network. A honeypot is a fake system and data that appear real to the adversary. Adversaries, who mistakenly attack honeypot systems, reveal their activity to the victim and exfiltrate useless data. Jump boxes are virtual airgaps that segment the network by instituting an additional layer of multifactor authentication and by restricting the number of authorized users. Virtual systems can be used to reduce internal costs and they can be configured to periodically self-terminate and redeploy from a saved disk image so that malware cannot remain on the system. The information security team can use beacons, tokens, or even malware to weaponize data against internal and external adversaries. These tools can also be used to trace exfiltrated data and to conduct network forensics after an incident. Finally, information about suspicious activity or active threats should be safely shared with law enforcement and with the community at large.

CONCLUSION

There will always be new adversaries, motivated by different philosophies, which possess more technical sophistication and stealth and attack new vulnerabilities with more evolved exploits, that are delivered along multiple layers and vectors. There are no silver bullet solutions that offer all-inclusive blanket protection from all threats. In our previous work, we've said that, "the only defense is a layered defense", and this statement holds true even in the face of defending against Cyber-Jihad. Layered security that detects, responds to, and predicts threats will continue to be the most viable technical tools in any meaningful cyber defense arsenal. The human element will continue to be the weakest element in cybersecurity; therefore, education that promotes cyber hygiene and a security centric organizational culture must be introduced and consistently reinforced at every level of every organization in every niche, and within every industry genre.

While many cyberterrorist organizations are lacking in their capacity to pose a significant cyber threat to global organizations, ISIS already possesses the motive, means, and opportunity to acquire the personnel and code necessary to begin launching devastating cyber campaigns. The

Cyber-Jihadist organization already possesses a complex communication infrastructure that it can leverage to rapidly train its forces to launch attacks. Moreover, the United Cyber Caliphate already declared an electronic jihad earlier this year. ISIS has the capacity to rapidly adopt ransomware and other malware to counteract the allied strategy targeting its fiscal assets. The malware can be used to inflict chaos, disruption, and loss on its enemies. Global organizations failed to improve their cyber postures when the Anthem and OPM breaches occurred. They lethargically procrastinate defending their networks until yet another catastrophic breach occurs. A renaissance in cybersecurity that evolves with the threat landscape must be injected into the very cultural DNA of American society in order to combat this omnipresent and persistent threat to our critical infrastructure, economy and national security.

PART 2

ICIT ANALYSIS:
THE WOUND COLLECTORS

PROFILING THE SELF RADICALIZED
LONE-WOLF TERRORIST

INTRODUCTION

The lone wolf is a self-radicalized, homegrown terrorist fueled by an extremist perspective of a distorted ideological variant. Whether they be Islamic Jihadists or far right/left anti-government activists, these contorted dogmatic mutations are merely a centralized point of focus for a deeper psycho-social affliction in the individual. Acts of domestic terrorism in the West are escalating at an alarming rate and due to the instant gratification provided by the internet and social media, there is no perspective, no matter how extreme, that is not readily available in the form of forum, chat or propaganda to the individual who ventures to find it. At this time, lone wolf attacks and attackers have sparked public, political and law enforcement curiosity due to the, seemingly, random and independent action of a self-radicalized extremist with modest or no ties directly to the group in which they proclaim the action to be dedicated. A more comprehensive understanding of the perplexing composition of the lone wolf is a mandatory prerequisite to creating lasting strategies to combat the escalation of this profound domestic threat. Certain events have garnered more media coverage, such as:

» September 2013, Aaron Alexis killed 12 people at the Washington Navy Yard

» November 2014, Larry McWilliams fired more than 100 rounds at four government buildings in Austin, Texas

» July 2015, John R. Houser killed two people and wounded nine others at a movie theater in Lafayette, Louisiana

» October 2015, Christopher Harper-Mercer killed 9 of his peers at Umpqua Community College in Oregon

» December 2015, Syed Rizwan Farook and Tashfeen Malik, husband and wife, killed 14 people at a holiday office party in San Bernardino, California

» June 2016, Omar Mateen killed 49 people and injured 53 others at the Pulse nightclub in Orlando, Florida.

All of these tragedies, and numerous others, were committed by troubled American citizens, against their own people, with little or no help from foreign influences. These threat actors were lone-wolves. The Georgetown University National Security Critical Issue Task Force (NSCITF) defines lone-wolf terrorism as: "The deliberate creation and exploitation of fear through violence or threat of violence committed by a single actor who pursues political change linked to a formulated ideology, whether his own or that of a larger organization, and who does not receive orders, direction, or material support from outside sources." Decades ago, radicals could be monitored through the group meetings they attended, the purchases that they made, and the information (blueprints, instruction books, etc.) that they sought. Now active membership in organized hate groups is in decline because the internet affords troubled minds a thick layer of anonymity and numerous websites, forums, and message boards, where they can self-radicalize and learn dangerous information. The Southern Poverty Law Center studied 63 incidents that occurred between April 2009 and February 2015, and found that a domestic terrorist attack or foiled attack occurred almost every 34 days and that lone-wolf threat actors were behind almost three-fourths of the attacks. Anti-government extremists perpetrated roughly half of the incidents, while white supremacists or Islamic extremists perpetrated the remainder. Lone-wolves join these communities and ideologies because they want to escape their lives and express their internal frustration, rage, and resentment, in service to a cause more meaningful than their existence. A lone-wolf threat actor is the result of a lifetime of hate, anger, and loneliness. Joe Navarro, one of the founders of the FBI's Behavioral Analysis Unit refers to lone-wolf extremists as "wound collectors". There are three distinct stages in their development: ideation, isolation, and action.

1 | DEVELOPMENT

EARLY DEVELOPMENT

Domestic terrorists are not the sole product of an ideology, of the mental health system, or of the American society; rather, they are the cumulative amalgamation of numerous contributing factors, congealed into a troubled mind, and expressed through acts of violence. Many, but not all, lone-wolf terrorists exhibit some, or all, of the following characteristics: a mental illness, anxiety, vocational problems, high-stress levels, problems with intimate partner relationships, social awkwardness, violent communications, and high intelligence. All lone-wolves lack empathy for their fellow humans. These tendencies develop over a lifetime, not an instant.

There is no definitive profile for lone-wolves; however, every lone-wolf lies on the same spectrum and exhibits some of the characteristics within the profile. Lone-wolf tendencies are the result of a lack of socialization and the formation of meaningful interpersonal relationships in early development. Often, this begins in early childhood or adolescence, with a poor home life. Sometimes one or both parents are physically or mentally abusive; in other cases, guardians are negligent. In either situation, their internal familial structure is weak and the child develops devoid of strong emotional attachments. The term "lone" is in lone-wolf for a reason beyond their independence in their actions. These threat actors have a history of being "loners," "quiet," or "losers." They are often remembered as uncharismatic silhouettes in the far corners of memories. Their detachment and lack of developed interpersonal skills makes them either the targets of schoolyard bullies or the bane of social crowds, often both. Their stunted development and their isolation often lead to emotional or psychiatric instability. The subject becomes comfortable with thoughts or acts of violence against themselves or others.

Developing lone-wolves used to retreat into their rooms or to isolated areas to escape the suffocating purgatory of their lives, until they were old enough to escape with all of their pent- up hatred. Now, these troubled minds turn to online communities, propaganda, and message boards, for immediate escape and acceptance. As a result of the ubiquity, availability, and pervasiveness of the internet, the age of lone-wolf threat actors is decreasing and they are entering the ideation stage earlier in life.

LATER DEVELOPMENT

The lone-wolf attacker often experiences four periods that cause them to enter the ideation stage after early development. First, they experience some form of grievance. This feeling of being persecuted, bullied, threatened, injured, or broken may stem from early development, or it may derive from disenfranchisement later in life. As a result, they experience depression as a form of restlessness, despair, or suicidal temptation. An unfreezing event, a crisis where there is perceived or experienced major loss, such as loss of relationship, loss of vocation, public humiliation, or failure or loss of status, causes them to project their grievances as an act of depression onto a manifested target and enter the ideation stage. Essentially, the severances of the connections that bind the individual to society leave them with little to lose; thereby freeing them to commit radical actions. Finally, usually before the cycle, or between the isolation and action stages, the subject familiarizes themselves with firearms and other weapons.

Background checks and other similar mechanisms have not yet prevented lone-wolves from legally obtaining firearms. Individuals like Mateen, who had neither a criminal past nor a record of diagnosed mental illness, are difficult to detect. Nevertheless, detection is not impossible.

The FBI investigated Mateen twice and interviewed him three times for connections to domestic terrorism. Mateen had a history of weapons training, he worked as an armed security guard, and he had applied to be a police officer. Even if he passed the check and was permitted to purchase the handgun and long gun that he did prior to the Pulse shooting, the check could have thrown up a red flag that would have informed law enforcement to watch his activity.

1. grievance
2. depression
3. energizing event
4. familiarizes with weapons

2 | THE STAGES OF LONE-WOLF DEVELOPMENT

IDEATION

Sixty-eight percent of lone-wolf attacks that occurred between April 2009 and February 2015 were conducted by males, between the ages of 20 and 49, and 59% used firearms that were legally purchased within two months of the attack. In contrast, violent criminals are typically within the age range of 15-24 years. The older range of ages suggests that the lone-wolves spend years absorbing radical ideology before finally turning belief into action and committing acts of violence. Due to the advent of the internet, potential threat actors have greater access to polarizing material that they can use to self-radicalize earlier and faster, which explains why recent threat actors have been younger than the range. Law enforcement has less time to detect, deter, or prevent lone-wolf activities on an individual basis. The availability of material and the permutations of jihadist and antigovernment ideologies means that law enforcement also must monitor *snip it in the bud at ideation stage*

significantly more threats across numerous additional channels and threat vectors. The most effective way to prevent threats from developing is for citizens and law enforcement to detect threats in the ideation stage and initiate monitoring or counter measures before the threat further develops.

The ideation stage begins with the development of a fixation on a specific grievance against a target who the subject feels harmed or committed an injustice against them. Often, the fixation is the projection of years of grievances and wounds onto a tangible target or target group who committed limited or no harm to the individual. Because the subject withholds internal anger or resentment from their development stage, they use the target as a manifested outlet and then they adopt an ideology or belief structure that allows them to rationalize those feelings against that target. Once they believe their own justification, they begin to spread the adopted views to their limited number of family or friends. In absence of either, the subject may contact strangers on the street or join a form of social activism (pamphletting, protesting, etc.) to extend their message. Those that they reach out to usually dismiss the ideas as nonsense, uncomfortable opinions, or idle banter. Consequently, the subject begins to withdraw and become less vocal with those in their lives. Eventually, the subject becomes physically or emotionally isolated.

as of august 2017

ISOLATION

christian is in this stage

The subject seeks an online community to validate their views. Once they find a website or forum to reinforce their vitriolic mentality, they begin a steep decline. Without a rational source, such as friends or family to dissuade or challenge the thoughts, the subject begins to actively communicate with likeminded individuals. Internal arguments within the community and oppositional forces cause the subject to become entrenched in their beliefs. As they self- radicalize online, efforts to detect or predict their activity become increasingly difficult because they move to different forums, transition to more secure communication channels, or migrate further into the deep net.

he doesn't have an affinity for computers

I don't see christian being this mobile

A two-year study of extremists conducted by the Intelligence Project iden-tified ten characteristics shared by killers who were active online. All of those monitored were unemployed or had difficulty holding employment. All engaged in a form of public activism at some point in their develop-ment. Many of the subjects had a history of domestic violence or incidents at their homes. Social science suggests that there may be a correlation be-tween domestic violence and lone-wolf attacks. An analysis of FBI data on mass shootings from 2009 to 2015, revealed that 16% of lone-wolf attack-ers, had a history of domestic violence.

Additionally, 57% of lone-wolf threat actors include at least one family member in their victims. Each subject posted on more than one message board, blog, or website. They frequented these channels for at least 18 months prior to their actions. On the sites, they exhibited antagonistic or argumentative behavior with other users. There was an increase or de-crease in their posting patterns in the months prior to the attacks. Each discussed violence as an acceptable and justified solution to their griev-ances. Weapons were also actively discussed. Finally, a specific "enemy," usually members of another race or the government, were identified as the source of their problems. Extremists in this state of mind develop a significant amount of anxiety and inner turmoil as their mind obsesses and fixates on their ideology and "enemy." Eventually, the only way to relieve the anxiety is to harm or kill someone.

ACTION

The subject may stew on their mental state for years or decades while they acquire weapons, scope out targets, and plan their attacks. The lone-wolf may delay action by victimizing friends and family or by perpetrating oth-er, smaller crimes. They may even convince others or themselves for a time that the plan is only a hypothetical expression of frustration upon which they will never act. At this stage, lone-wolf threat actors are nearly ready to cause serious harm. Ironically, this is also the most difficult time to de-tect their intent. It is the responsibility of friends, family members, and others to report indications of an impending incident to law enforcement instead of dismissing or discounting individuals who try to recruit or who try to preemptively justify their actions. For instance, Omar Mateen's second wife, Noor Salman reportedly knew of her husband's plans and may have even helped him scope out venues to attack. If she had reported his activities to law enforcement, then 49 deaths and 53 injuries could have been prevented.

3 | CONTRIBUTING FACTORS

IDEOLOGY

S Lone-wolf threat actors are not solely driven by ideology. Eliminating ideology will not prevent lone-wolf attacks. Ideology is simply the outlet that the internal radicalization is expressed through. Ideology does provide a sense of self and a sense of purpose that troubled individuals have difficulty finding in other facets of their lives. Ideology can act as a social motivator that polarizes the individual to act on internal biases and hatred. Ideology does not cause an impairment of will. In most cases, the lone-wolf actor has a stronger will than the majority of devout followers of an ideology; this is because the lone-wolf is using the ideology as a vehicle to justify their actions rather than a crutch to find a sense of greater purpose or meaning.

Without the specific ideology such as conspiracy theories, Islam, racism, etc., the threat actor would find another channel to slowly turn than passion into hatred into terrible action. Across the globe, there are approximately 1.2 billion Muslims and 2 billion Christians. Of each group, a few hundred thousand members carry radical views. Of that small percentage, only a fraction of a fraction commits violent acts because they recognize that opinions are cheap, opinions are numerous, and that such actions are costly, disruptive, and likely violate the tenets of their religion.

MENTAL HEALTH

There is a substantial gap between belief and action. A significant number, but not all, lone-wolf threat actors suffer from diagnosable mental illnesses. Common symptoms are anger control problems, obsession, depression, and suicidal thoughts or tendencies. The threat posed by lone-wolf activists can be reduced by collecting better intelligence and training law enforcement more effectively, but it can also be reduced by improving our behavioral health system and increasing the quality and availability of those services. A severely troubled individual capable of lone-wolf attacks is in the most need of access to high quality, non- stigmatized behavioral health and ancillary services when they experience the violent or isolationist tendencies that lead to self-radicalization. Only a minority of people with mental illnesses are even remotely violent; however, some studies have indicated that within terrorist populations, a larger percentage of lone wolf terrorists are found to be mentally ill than group- oriented terrorists. Mental health patients sometimes describe their actions after the fact as compelling delusions, citing phrases such as "I was not myself" or "I was out of my mind." Lone- wolf threat actors do not exhibit this characteristic. They premeditate, plan, and execute their agendas. This demonstrates that mental health is not the cause of their actions, but like ideology and access to weapons, is merely a contributing factor in the puzzle that is the mind of a lone-wolf threat actor.

PROPAGANDA

Jihadist propaganda and anti-government manifestos convince troubled individuals to believe that they can be the sole soldier who turns the tides of war, exposes the great evil, or strikes a devastating blow to the enemy. As a result, lone wolf attacks are conducted on behalf of the cause without direction or communication with the group. The jihadist propaganda machine is well resourced and ubiquitous across social media and the internet. Its propaganda calls for lone-wolf actions, glorifying the actions by deluding troubled minds into believing that they can serve a greater cause through their actions and thereby have a meaningful impact on a community that wants and accepts them. Racist and anti-government militants are similarly attracted to numerous conspiracy message boards, publications, and sites for the self-gratifying communities of fellow isolationists who congregate there.

Researchers at the University of Miami studied second-by-second longitudinal records of online support for ISIS propaganda since its formation in 2014. They found that lone wolf supporters only remained alone for a few weeks at most before they were drawn into larger communities, referred to as aggregates. They studied 196 pro-ISIS aggregates consisting of over 108,086 individual followers between January 1, 2015 and August 31, 2015. By the end of August, the number of lone wolf and aggregate participants numbered 134,857. With their data, the researchers were able to model the propaganda transfer network and discern a few preliminary conclusions. Anti-ISIS agencies can prevent the formation of large pro-ISIS online groups by breaking up smaller ones. If anti-ISIS agencies are not active or not active enough, ISIS support grows exponentially into super aggregates of smaller groups. Further, When ISIS networks are not fragmented fast enough, a piece of propaganda can spread at a rate proportional to the speed of the channel times the probability of follower-to-follower transmission, divided by the rate of follower recovery. The rate of fragmentation must exceed this ratio to prevent the diffusion of materials. Essentially, by actively targeting small aggregate communities before they merge into larger communities, law enforcement can combat threats. They can stymie the polarization of lone-wolf threat actors and they can preempt the formation of resilient complex terror networks.

The most effective mechanism for limiting lone-wolf activism is to restrict access to the propaganda online. Anonymous and US Cyber Command are already conducting cyberattacks against ISIS's infrastructure. Jihadist Twitter accounts, forums, and communication channels are likewise targeted. The State Department has also started to empower those living in the affected regions to launch counter-propaganda campaigns to dispel the allure surrounding ISIS. The United States has also targeted ISIS's financial resources to reduce its ability to pay its fighters. The combination of these efforts have reduced ISIS's recruitment and its distribution of propaganda; however, propaganda is cheap, the internet is vast, and lone-wolf threat actors are waiting for the right cause to lure them to action. As long as extremist organizations such as ISIS or anti-government movements exist, they will continue to produce propaganda and infect the minds of troubled individuals.

Those seduced by jihadist or anti-government propaganda are troubled individuals who are desperate for a sense of purpose, a community, or an escape from their internal or external conflict. These individuals want to feel important in some way. They want to justify their hatred, bias, or resentment through a cause larger than themselves, within a community of peers. In a sense, they crave the literal power that they feel when they choose a target and plan the attack. They crave the euphoria over the decision of who lives and who dies, because it affords them a level of control that they do not have in their average life. Prior to extreme self-radicalization, lone-wolf attackers tend to adopt an affinity for weapons and the power that they associate with them.

CONCLUSION

The new landscape of warfare is a convergence of the cyber and the physical. One side will fight for a perversion of extremist ideology; the other side will fight for its right to exist. Digitized information warfare and propaganda will be used in unison with scattershot lone wolf attacks by one opponent while the larger more technologically sophisticated side will continue to depend on traditional outdated mechanisms of combat that yield inferior results. This new war will be fought on the terms of highly maneuverable techno-guerrillas while world power giants clumsily fumble about as old alliances crumble and new powers are erected by sheer will, and a willingness to do anything and everything necessary in order to achieve a distorted version of global domination.

This new war is first and foremost a battle for the mind of a psycho-archetype that is fueled by propaganda that will satisfy all ranges of rhetorical intrigue and violent curiosity. This propaganda, packaged and delivered via all layers of cyberspace, is calibrated with the intention to steer the mentally unstable, socially isolated and emotionally fractured target toward an ideology with the aim to capitalize off this malicious insider who is ready to consummate the violent threats that they have broadcasted to family, friends and virtual peers. Lone wolf actors pose the most devastating insider threat to the general population at large.

What is the solution to the conundrum of federal "bureaucracy paralysis" whose totem pole chain of power creates the illusion of action while the individual's lack of action is camouflaged in the chain of command? State sponsored theatrics such as signs stating "If you see something, say something" do little more than cultivate the illusion of security and introduce new elements of paranoia that only distract law enforcement attention from investigating those with true telltale signs of an active threat. An update in general law enforcement education, the localized and federal monitoring of online activity by those on forums that truly pose a threat to national security and a revolution in meaningful threat sharing are the embryonic starting point for erecting defenses that truly combat the lone wolf threat.

PART 3

AMERICAN ISIS

ANALYSIS OF THE ORLANDO
JIHADIST & LONE-WOLF ATTACKS

ISIS lone wolves are being activated in towns and cities globally for the most potent cyber-physical combination of guerrilla attack ever to be introduced in modern warfare. This new enemy, fueled by extremist ideology, defies traditional profiling attributes such as race, sex, age, education, occupation and nationality. At 2:00 a.m. on Sunday, June 13, 2016, police dispatchers received a call from a man, now identified as Omar Mateen, pledging his allegiance and his actions to the Islamic State of Iraq and Syria (ISIS). Omar Mateen fired over 110 rounds from an AR-15 assault rifle into to the LGBTQ+ crowd of the Pulse nightclub in Orlando Florida, in a lone wolf attack conducted on behalf of ISIS, against Western society. In the confined space of the nightclub, 50 individuals were killed and another 53 were wounded. One in three patrons of Pulse, were injured or killed in the three hour incident that will be remembered as the worst act of terrorism on American soil since September 11, 2001 and the deadliest assault on the LGBTQ+ community in American history. Hours after the attack, ISIS claimed responsibility for Mateen's actions on their Amaq News Agency application. Following Mateen's actions, ISIS called for more lone-wolf attacks across the globe against LGBTQ+ communities and they began posting images and videos of the bodies of homosexual men and women killed by ISIS throughout their reign of terror. Rather than allow ISIS to increase its renown and thereby its influence, the focus on this incident should be on the victims, on the recovery of the nation, and on ensuring that events like these will never happen again. Unfortunately, to accomplish these goals and to prevent similar incidents in the future, law enforcement and legislators must expedite their currently vague comprehension of the shooter's ideology, of the nature of lone- wolf attacks, and of the circumstances that led to this tragedy.

ISIS was originally formed as an Iraqi branch of Al Qaeda in 2004, but It has since developed into an independent organization that is more radical in its views and more technologically sophisticated in its use of social media and the internet than Al Qaeda. In summer 2014, ISIS leader Abu Bakr al-Baghdadi declared a global jihad. He called on all Muslims to join his cause by either travelling to Iraq or Syria or by supporting the jihad locally, by terrorizing "Western Crusaders" in their homelands. ISIS has a strong social media presence that heavily recruits and promotes "lone-wolf" actions on conventional social media such as Twitter, Facebook, and Tumblr, and on less conventional channels such as forums and message boards. Members target lonely and misguided individuals, regardless of their initial beliefs, by offering a sense of community and by glamorizing the fight, actions, and lifestyle of the movement. These angry, social outcasts are ideal lone-wolves due to their isolation, initiative, and lack of empathy.

The Georgetown National Security Critical Issue Task Force (NSCITF) defines lone wolf attacks as, "The deliberate creation and exploitation of fear through violence or threat of violence committed by a single actor who pursues political change linked to a formulated ideology, whether his own or that of a larger organization, and who does not receive orders, direction, or material support from outside sources." Similar to Omar Mateen and the assault on Pulse, in December 2015, Syed Rizwan Farook and Tashfeen Malik shot 14 people at a holiday party in San Bernardino, California on behalf of ISIS. The pair never made direct contact with ISIS leadership; instead, inspired by propaganda and the call for lone-wolf attacks, the couple self-radicalized. Lone-wolf attacks, such as the Orlando or San Bernardino shootings, combine personal motives with the agendas of extremist ideologies. This is shown in the attacker's deliberate choice of target and the minimal direct support that they receive from the terrorist organization prior to the attack. Lone-wolf attacks, such as the Pulse tragedy, are the result of imminent insider threats within the nation. ISIS has regularly published lists of targets online and in their publications and called to foreign jihadists to conduct lone-wolf attacks within Western nations. In a March

2016 statement, ISIS declared to foreign sympathizers, "The smallest action you do in their heartland is better and more enduring to us than what you would if you were with us." "If one of you hoped to reach the Islamic State, we wish we were in your place to punish the Crusaders day and night," the message reportedly added. ISIS usually claims that the lists of names, addresses, and other information were obtained from a data breach or insider threat; however, the information almost always can be traced to open source intelligence. In April 2016, ISIS published a "kill-list" on the secure messaging application, Telegram, with over 8,000 names, mostly American citizens. At least 600 of those on the list were Florida residents. Three days prior to the Pulse assault, FBI agent-turned lawyer Stuart Kaplan allegedly warned that the list was going to inspire lone-wolf attacks. Law enforcement was aware of the threat posed by the ISIS "kill-lists"; however, there was little that they could do. They could expend significant resources protecting every person listed, but the lists are meant to inspire attacks against anyone, not necessarily the specific targets listed. Signal intelligence does not predict lone-wolf attacks because there is a strong likelihood that the attacker either never communicated with the extremist group or that they encrypted their communications to hide their activity.

It is impossible to know what ideology, biases, or hatred, an individual truly believes; consequently, it is very difficult to identify lone-wolf extremists prior to their attacks. ISIS has a very powerful social media presence and propaganda machine. According to the Brookings Institute, around 50 persistent personnel operate thousands of ISIS twitter accounts and Telegram channels. ISIS conveys news and information through its social media and through its mobile applications, Dawn of Glad Tidings and Amaq Agency. ISIS also distributes publications, such as Dabiq and Kybernetiq, through Pastebin and Justpaste.it. Dabiq is a monthly 30-80 page publication that promotes ISIS's ideology, praises suicide bombers and lone-wolf attackers, like Mateen, and glorifies the brutality of the jihadist cause. Past issues of Dabiq have featured multipage spreads glorifying those behind the 2015 Paris attacks, such as Abdelhamid Abaaoud, and the San Bernardino shooters, Syed Rizwan Farook and Tashfeen Malik. The next issue will likely feature Omar Mateen. ISIS may use the attack to radicalize additional lone-wolf attackers and to inspire copycat incidents. ISIS uses the Kybernetiq publication to train radicals in operational security and secure communications. It is possible that in the future, the publication will be used to train a jihadist cyber-army to conduct attacks against Western organizations.

Groups like ISIS train their members to blend into the surrounding society. ISIS even adapted and released an Al Qaeda manual, "Safety and Security Guidelines for Lone-Wolf Mujahideen", to train its affiliates to avoid detection. The manual recommends that lone- wolves blend into society by "Westernizing" their appearance, shaving their beards, and through, polite, concise dialogue. It is unclear whether Mateen read the manual, as he was born and raised in the United States, but one coincidence stands out. The manual recommends that lone-wolves carry out their attacks in night clubs due to the environment of distraction from loud music and the dense crowds of people.

According to the media, Omar Mateen was born in New York City in 1987 to Afghani parents who immigrated to the United States in 1980. Mateen lived in Fort Pierce, Florida, where he worked as a security guard at G4S since 2007. He previously worked as a correctional officer at a juvenile correction agency and he once sought admission to a police academy. According to the Federal Bureau of Alcohol, Tobacco, Firearms, and Explosives, Mateen legally purchased a rifle and a pistol within a week or two of the Pulse massacre. It is now obvious that Mateen posed a severe threat to his fellow citizens; however, he, like any lone-wolf attacker, was able to blend in. Mateen passed multiple background checks for his position at the correction agency, his application to the police academy, and his position as an armed security guard. Law enforcement and legislators need to recognize certain aspects of his example. Skilled lone-wolf attackers do not display signs of their skewed ideology or premeditated actions. Though Mateen was of Middle-Eastern heritage, not all lone-wolf threat actors can be identified via physical attribute; nor should they be. According to defectors and based on a small sample size of 4,000 leaked records, ISIS recruits at least 1.15% of its active, local members from the United States. Around 87.4% of ISIS recruits were born between 1980 and 1999, with an average age of 28. The backgrounds of those recruited, who did not migrate to ISIS occupied regions varies more intensely. FBI arrest reports indicate that the profile ranges from black men in Minnesota to white women in North

Carolina, to isolated teenagers in homes across the nation. The power behind ideology and nationalism is that it transcends metrics like age and skin tone. Ideas are infectious and can be poisonous if whispered into the right ears.

Mateen's self-radicalization did not go entirely unnoticed. The FBI investigated him in 2013 after he made comments to coworkers suggesting that he had ties to terrorist communities. According to Ronald Hopper, the assistant agent in charge of the FBI's Tampa division, he was investigated again in 2014 for a possible connection to Moner Mohammad Abu Salha, the first American suicide bomber in Syria. Abu Salha was a member of the Al Qaeda affiliated group, Jabhat al- Nusra. Neither investigation revealed solid evidence that Mateen had tangible connections to terrorist networks. The FBI's inability to connect the shooter to ISIS is not surprising. The extremist group has a thriving online presence that teaches its members how to obfuscate their communications and how to blend into the surrounding culture until they launch their attacks. In total, Mateen was interviewed at least 3 times. His lone-wolf tendencies were not discovered because lone-wolf threats do not display the conventional signs of terrorism. They self-radicalize or operate with only limited direction from extremist groups such as ISIS. In a sense, they blindly serve the cause, not the organization. This makes them ideal foreign recruits for ISIS because propaganda and media coverage are enough to catalyze their self-radicalization.

Omar Mateen had a history of violence and hatred. One former co-worker recounts that Mateen often talked about killing people and he expressed open hatred of gays, blacks, women, and Jews. His former wife, Sitora Yusefiy, told journalists that he had a history of steroid abuse, that he would regularly "express hatred towards everything," and that he physically abused her until she was rescued by family. She describes Mateen as "emotionally unstable," "mentally ill," and bipolar. Similarly, the Imam of the Florida mosque where Mateen attended for nearly a decade, described him as unusually quiet, supposedly aggressive, and socially dissociated from the community. The ISIS recruitment profile is a carbon copy of Omar Mateen's life. ISIS relies on isolated, psychologically unstable and angry individuals who can be persuaded to devote their lives to a radical ideology and plan and launch attacks against their fellow citizens. Mateen is not and will not be the sole lone-wolf attacker. Other lonely and disenfranchised individuals sit behind televisions, keyboards, and mobile devices across the nation.

Lone-wolf attacks inspire a culture of fear, distrust, and xenophobia upon which extremist groups like ISIS thrive. In response to the attack, President Obama said in a special address from the White House, "In the face of hate and violence, we will love one another. We will not give in to fear or turn against each other. Instead, we will stand united as Americans to protect our people and defend our nation, and to take action against those who threaten us." ISIS relies on its propaganda and publications to poison the troubled minds of some Western citizens and turn them into insider threats against their nation. As coverage of the attacks and ISIS's renown grows, the nation becomes more polarized and more fragmented. As heated discussions take place over the coming days and month about the recent attack, more individuals become internally radicalized towards ISIS's ideology, and more lone-wolf attacks increase as a result. At this time, our Nation needs to combat the lone-wolf threat by dissuading ISIS's influence on our discussion, by recognizing the symptoms that lead people towards the militant communities, by remaining united against the terrorist threat and consciously communicating the message to legislators that this is not a time for knee jerk reactive legislation that diminishes constitutional and civil rights. Rather, explicit action rooted in sound comprehension of this uniquely malicious threat is the only way to introduce viable legislation that combats the quintessence of the threat.

CONTACT INFORMATION

Legislative and Federal Agency Inquiries:

- Parham Eftekhari, Senior Fellow, ICIT (parham@icitech.org, 202-600-7250 ext 101)

Links:

Website: www.icitech.org

Twitter: https://twitter.com/ICITorg

LinkedIn: https://www.linkedin.com/company/
institute-for-critical-infrastructure-technology- icit-

Facebook: https://www.facebook.com/ICITorg

SOURCES

PART 1 SOURCES:

Al Alarabiya English:

> http://english.alarabiya.net/en/views/news/middle-east/2016/05/18/
> Fundamentalism-and- the-digital-era.html

The Atlantic

> http://www.theatlantic.com/international/archive/2014/06/
> isis-iraq-twitter-social-media- strategy/372856/

Bat Blue:

> http://www.batblue.com/bat-blue-special-report-terror-goes-cyber/

BBC:

> http://www.bbc.com/news/world-middle-east-27838034

> http://www.bbc.com/news/world-africa-13809501

BGR:

http://bgr.com/2016/04/28/isis-united-cyber-caliphate-hackers/

Birmingham Mail:

http://www.birminghammail.co.uk/news/midlands-news/
isis-terrorist-junaid-hussain- killed-10069425

Bitcoinist:

http://bitcoinist.net/cerber-ransomware-as-a-service/ Blasting News:

http://us.blastingnews.com/news/2016/03/the-islamic-state-targets-
nj-transit-police-on- social-media-00855979.html

http://www.bleepingcomputer.com/news/security/the-cerber-ran-
somware-not-only- encrypts-your-data-but-also-speaks-to-you/

Bleeping Computer:

http://www.bleepingcomputer.com/news/security/the-cerber-ran-
somware-not-only- encrypts-your-data-but-also-speaks-to-you/

Brica:

https://brica.de/alerts/alert/public/940056/
islamic-state-launches-the-kybernetiq- magazine-for-cyber-jihadists/

The Brookings Institute:

http://www.brookings.edu/~/media/research/files/papers/2015/03/
isis-twitter-census- berger-morgan/isis_twitter_census_berger_mor-
gan.pdf.

Business Insider:

http://www.businessinsider.com/isis-supporter-outlines-how-to-
support-terror-group- with-bitcoin-2014-7?IR=T

Cloudflare:

http://blog.cloudflare.com/the-ddos-that-almost-broke-the-internet

CSC:

http://blogs.csc.com/2016/02/04/
breaking-down-the-threat-of-cyber-terrorism/

CNN Money:

http://money.cnn.com/2015/10/15/technology/isis-energy-grid/ CSO
Online:

http://www.csoonline.com/article/3040619/security/cerber-ransom-
ware-sold-as-a- service-speaks-to-victims.html

Cyber Orient:

http://www.cyberorient.net/article.do?articleId=9538 Defcon 21:

http://youtu.be/q2FxTgd3uTE?t=24m7s Express:

http://www.express.co.uk/news/world/617977/ISIS-Cyber-Caliphate-
Hack-Twitter- Saudi-Arabia-Britain-Terror-Tony-McDowell-Junaid-
Hussain

Financial Times:

http://www.ft.com/cms/s/0/d05da464-20d4-11e6-aa98- db1e-
01fabc0c.html#axzz4A9pRmnVS

FireEye:

https://www.fireeye.com/blog/threat- research/2016/05/cerber_ran-
somware_partners_with_Dridex.html

Flashpoint:

https://www.flashpoint-intel.com/news/flashpoint-issues-new-re-
port-demonstrating- advancement-of-isis-organized-cyber-capabili-
ties/

Foreign Affairs:

https://www.foreignaffairs.com/articles/syria/2016-05-01/quitting-
isis Free Beacon:

http://freebeacon.com/national-security/pentagon-isis-has-almost-same-number-of- members-as-when-u-s-airstrikes-began/#

http://freebeacon.com/national-security/cyber-caliphate-hackers-not-linked-to-islamic- state/

Free Malaysia Today:

http://www.freemalaysiatoday.com/category/world/2016/05/15/efforts-to-counter-is- propaganda-bear-fruit-experts-say/

F-Secure:

https://www.f-secure.com/documents/996508/1030745/blacken-ergy_whitepaper.pdf. https://www.f-secure.com/v-descs/backdoor_w32_blackenergy.shtml

The Guardian:

http://www.theguardian.com/world/2015/apr/12/isis-cyber-caliphate-hacking-technology- arms-race

Helpnet Security:

https://www.helpnetsecurity.com/2016/05/24/cerber-ransomware-ddos/ IB Times:

http://www.ibtimes.co.uk/cerber-terrifying-russian-ransomware-speaks-bitcoin-demand- blackmail-victims-out-loud-1547592

http://www.ibtimes.co.uk/isis-hackers-infiltrate-ministry-defence-threaten-leak-secret- intelligence-1558092

http://www.ibtimes.co.uk/isis-24-7-helpdesk-terror-encryption-hot-line-teaches- cybersecurity-1529328

http://www.ibtimes.co.uk/isis-launches-cyberwar-maga-zine-jihadists-making-1536334 http://www.ibtimes.co.uk/are-isis-hackers-trying-destroy-internet-1533332

http://www.ibtimes.co.uk/john-mcafee-massive-ddos-attack-inter-net-was-smartphone- botnet-popular-app-1532993

http://www.ibtimes.co.uk/

wont-pay-no-problem-cerber-ransomware-adds-your-pc- botnet-send-out-ddos-attacks-1561552

Kaspersky:

https://blog.kaspersky.com/billion-dollar-apt-carbanak/7519/
Malwarebytes:

https://blog.malwarebytes.org/threat-analysis/2016/03/
cerber-ransomware-new-but- mature/

https://blog.malwarebytes.org/cybercrime/2016/04/
magnitude-ek-malvertising-campaign- adds-fingerprinting-gate/

Market Watch:

http://www.marketwatch.com/story/
how-vulnerable-are-the-us-stock-markets-to-hackers- 2015-07-31

McAfee:

https://blogs.mcafee.com/mcafee-labs/blackenergy_ukrai-nian_power_grid/ https://blogs.mcafee.com/mcafee-labs/
updated-blackenergy-trojan-grows-more-powerful/

National Counterterrorism Center:

https://www.nctc.gov/site/groups/al_shabaab.html

NBC News:

http://www.nbcnews.com/storyline/paris-terror-attacks/
isis-has-help-desk-terrorists- staffed-around-clock-n464391

NPR:

http://www.npr.org/2016/04/25/475631277/
isis-uses-cyber-capabilities-to-attack-the-u-s- online

PC Magazine:

http://www.pcmag.com/article2/0,2817,2453157,00.asp Security
Affairs:

http://securityaffairs.co/wordpress/28300/cyber-crime/isis-cyber-caliphate.html

https://securelist.com/blog/research/68732/the-great-bank-robbery-the-carbanak-apt/

Security Intelligence:

https://securityintelligence.com/the-threat-is-coming-from-inside-the-network/ Scientific American:

http://www.scientificamerican.com/article/how-u-s-cyber-bombs-against-terrorists-really- work/

Spamhaus:

http://www.spamhaus.org/organization/ The Star:

https://www.thestar.com/news/world/2016/05/30/the-daesh-files-database-provides- snapshot-of-recruits.html

Syrian Economic Forum:

http://www.syrianef.org/En/2015/09/in-the-arab-region-syria-comes-in-first-in- unemployment-with-more-than-12-million-unem-ployed/

Telegeography:

http://global-internet-map-2012.telegeography.com/ The Telegraph:

http://www.telegraph.co.uk/technology/2016/04/07/us-government-declares-cyber-war- on-isil/

http://www.telegraph.co.uk/technology/internet-security/12007170/Islamic-States- detailed-security-manual-reveals-its-cyber-strategy.html

The Times of Israel:

http://www.timesofisrael.com/anonymous-takes-war-against-tech-savvy-is-online/ Trend Micro:

http://blog.trendmicro.com/trendlabs-security-intelligence/ killdisk-and-blackenergy-are- not-just-energy-sector-threats/

http://www.trendmicro.com/vinfo/us/secu- rity/news/cybercrime-and-digital- threats/ cryptxxx-and-cerber-ransomware-get-major-updates

The Washington Post:

https://www.washingtonpost.com/news/worldviews/wp/2015/06/09/ the-islamic-state-or- someone-pretending-to-be-it-is-trying-to-raise- funds-using-bitcoin/

PART 2 SOURCES:

CBS News:

http://www.cbsnews.com/news/orlando-shooting-omar-mateen- father-seddique- mateen-taliban-god-punish-gays/

Mother Board:

http://motherboard.vice.com/read/what-is-a-lone-wolf-terrorist

New York Times:

http://www.nytimes.com/2016/06/16/world/americas/control-and- fear-what-mass- killings-and-domestic-violence-have-in-common. html?rref=us

http://www.nytimes.com/interactive/2015/10/03/us/how-mass- shooters-got-their- guns.html?_r=0

Psychology Today:

https://www.psychologytoday.com/blog/stop-the-cycle/201501/ lone-wolf-terrorists- and-mental-illness

https://www.psychologytoday.com/blog/the-modern-mind/201410/ the-making-lone- wolf-terrorist

Taylor and Francis Online: http://www.tandfonline.com/doi/abs/10.1 080/19434472.2015.1070189

Terrorism Analysts:

http://www.terrorismanalysts.com/pt/index.php/pot/article/ view/240

University of Maryland:

https://www.start.umd.edu/publication/toward-profile-lone-wolf-terrorists-what- moves-individual-radical-opinion-radical-action

YouTube:

https://www.youtube.com/watch?v=M7tpWFF0KtQ

https://www.youtube.com/watch?v=FI8ANFm3p1s

https://www.youtube.com/watch?v=dytL0a5YePw

PART 3 SOURCES:

ICIT: The Anatomy of Cyber Jihad

http://icitech.org/icit-brief-the-anatomy-of-cyber-jihad-cyberspace-is-the-new-great-equalizer/

Breitbart:

http://www.breitbart.com/national-security/2016/05/24/ramadan-violence-islamic-state-urges-lone- wolf-attacks-in-u-s-europe/

Daily Mail:

http://www.dailymail.co.uk/news/article-3638446/ISIS-posted-kill-list-online-inspire-lone-wolf-attacks- against-thousands-Americans-including-600-Florida.html

RT:

https://www.rt.com/news/328582-isis-lone-wolf-terrorist-manual/

Slate:

   http://www.slate.com/articles/news_and_politics/foreign-
   ers/2016/06/lone_wolf_terrorists_like_omar_ mateen_present_a_dif-
   ferent_kind_of_threat.html

Telegraph:

   http://www.telegraph.co.uk/news/2016/06/13/
   orlando-shooting-isil-wages-war-on-gays-in-the-west- after-omar-m/

Wall Street Journal:

   http://www.wsj.com/articles/
   islamic-state-urges-lone-wolf-attacks-in-the-west-1465773874

Made in the USA
Columbia, SC
25 May 2017